PRAISE FOR
PROFIT FIRST
for Minority Business Enterprises

"If you want to turn your business into a profitable money-making machine, *Profit First* by Susanne Mariga is exactly what you need to level-up your business operations. Her book lays out a winning system to build your dream business."

—MELINDA EMERSON, "SmallBizLady"
and author of *Fix Your Business*

"Anyone, Susanne counsels, can change the legacy they have inherited and become the first-generation financial success story in their family. **Highly recommended for fans of** Michelle Singletary, Patrice Washington, Tiffany Aliche, David Bach, and Suze Orman"

—*BlueInk Review*

"A vigorous and highly readable plan for building the finances of a new business."

—*Kirkus Reviews*

PROFIT
FIRST

— *FOR* —

Minority Business Enterprises

TRANSFORM YOUR MINORITY BUSINESS ENTERPRISE FROM
A CASH-EATING MONSTER TO A MONEY-MAKING MACHINE

Profit First for Minority Business Enterprises
By Susanne Mariga, CPA
The Avant-Garde Project, LLC, Houston, Texas
Copyright © 2021 The Avant-Garde Project, LLC
All Rights Reserved
ISBN 13: 978-1-7357759-0-6 (trade paperback)
ISBN 13: 978-1-7357759-1-3 (eBook)
Library of Congress Control Number: 2021910002
All trademarks and registered trademarks are the
property of their respective owners.
Book Design by CB Messer
Printed in the United States of America

10 9 8 7 6 5 4 3 2 1

This book is for informational purposes only. Information
contained within should not be considered legal, financial, or tax
advice. You should consult with your attorney or tax professional
to determine the best course of action for your business.

Mariga CPA PLLC does not make any guarantee of results from the use of
the content in this book. This publication is sold with the understanding
that neither Mariga CPA PLLC nor its publisher is engaged in rendering
legal, investment, or other professional services. If you require legal or other
expert assistance, you should seek the services of a competent professional.

To protect the innocent, some names have been changed.

To my children, Florence and Emmanuel.
Thank you for giving me the courage to take the leap
into entrepreneurship and the fortitude never to accept
the limits that the world would place upon me.

CONTENTS

NDATENDA!

("Thank you!" in Shona)

I HAVE COMMITTED A PERCENTAGE of the proceeds from this book to education for girls in Zimbabwe. Your purchase of this book enables us to change the legacy of many young girls in Zimbabwe by sending them to school.

Unemployment in Zimbabwe is very high. It is estimated that more than 75% of the population survives on informal trading, which makes it difficult for most parents to afford to send their children to primary and secondary school. Historically, the government has provided support in the form of grants and scholarships to college-bound students; however, parents are responsible for paying for their children's education until they get to the college level. Unfortunately, some students are left behind because of their financial situation and are unable to afford primary and secondary school fees.

The cause of girls' education has always been important to me, especially that of African girls, whose parents are sometimes left to choose between sending a daughter or son to school. Typically, sons are given the opportunity to pursue their education while daughters must stay at home to help with chores and care for the rest of the siblings. In extreme instances, girls are forced into early marriages. Our goal is to empower as many girls as we can by giving them an opportunity to pursue their education.

When we allow young women to receive an education, we not only alter their future, we pivot the future of their offspring for generations to come. Education allows young women to create their own destiny.

So, when you purchase *Profit First for Minority Business Enterprises,* you contribute to life-altering education for Zimbabwean girls. Thank you for being part of our mission to change legacies.

~ Susanne Mariga

FOREWORD

by Mike Michalowicz

THE MURDER OF GEORGE FLOYD on May 25, 2020, was a result of incessant, toxic prejudice. I realize that, as a white male, I cannot begin to comprehend the depth of pain and prejudice so many African American and other people of color have experienced. I cannot begin to comprehend the depth of toxicity, fear, and unwavering inequality that minority business owners are forced to live with. I cannot even begin to comprehend the inhumanity experienced by humanity. But I do believe it can be changed.

I asked my long-term friend and colleague, Susanne Mariga, if I could write the foreword for her book. My focus is small business. I love our institution endlessly. I want to serve all entrepreneurs. I want to eradicate entrepreneurial poverty. I don't believe that George Floyd's life, nor the lives that have been lost before and after his due to racial inequality, will be in vain. Change is afoot. A facilitator, or more likely *the* facilitator, of equity and inclusion is wealth. That's exactly what this book in your hands will create for you and all minority business enterprises (MBEs).

Susanne Mariga knows the MBE community because she is a minority business owner herself. Susanne is the child of an African-American mother from North Carolina who comes from a legacy of sharecroppers and slavery. Susanne's father is Chinese, and has also witnessed firsthand the inequities faced by people of color. Even though Susanne's father graduated magna cum laude in the 1970s, none of the Big Eight accounting firms would hire him because "his accent was too thick."

Against the odds, Susanne rose up. Susanne was the first Black woman in her family to graduate from college. She was the first female family member to become a Certified Public Accountant. She was the first to work at a Big Four accounting firm. She was the first to start a business. She was the first to write a book. Unfortunately, she was not the first, nor the last, to experience racism. She had to learn to navigate rooms where no one would look at her. She had to disregard muttered words and condescending glances. And she had to build a business in a context where people deliberately didn't work with her... not because of her capabilities, but because of her skin.

She started her accounting firm while on maternity leave, with $500. $500 of her own money. No golden parachute from her past employer. No money from family. No prior legacy.

Against the odds, Susanne grew an accounting practice that was recognized as a Goldman Sachs 10,000 Small Business and received the E-10 Award from the Houston Minority Supplier Development Council. And she is the first person in her family lineage to become a millionaire. She is a gen-one millionaire, and intends for you to gain that notable achievement too.

You too may be working against the odds. There is no question that you have the drive, the passion, and the talent to grow a wildly successful business. But you also experience forms of racism and oppression. You may wrestle with success guilt, which pressures you to hire friends and family. No matter what, you are busting through the stereotypes that have been thrust upon you. It takes immense bravery to recreate who you are and embrace what you really want in the very public way that entrepreneurship requires.

When I wrote *Profit First*, I wrote it to teach a system for achieving wealth. Susanne has taken *Profit First for Minority Business Enterprises* to an entirely new level. This is not only a book about a proven system for generating entrepreneurial wealth; it is also a system for shifting your mindset. You will learn to think differently, to manage your taxes differently, and to position yourself differently in order to achieve every facet of entrepreneurial wealth.

The information you will learn in this book has never before been so succinctly and coherently presented. This book has everything you need to achieve your financial objectives for your MBE and yourself.

I couldn't be prouder of Susanne Mariga and the extra-ordinary work she has put into making this knowledge available to you. MBEs will rise, and Susanne is going to start with you. Change is afoot, my friend, change is afoot.

INTRODUCTION

JANE HARRIS IS A BEAUTIFUL, creative, smart, hardworking Nigerian-American woman. Prior to starting The Virgin Hair Fantasy wig line, she worked at a shoe store. Shortly after she was promoted to manager, she transferred from Atlanta to New York. The pressure is intense for a soul working on Fifty-third Street and Madison Avenue, right in the middle of everything fashion. Jane felt good about her appearance—except for her hair. Limited in the hairstyles she could wear due to the length and natural texture of her hair, Jane felt she needed a wig, but she couldn't afford the one she wanted.

The wigs that caught Jane's eye cost $2,000—each. With no prior experience or formal cosmetology training, she went on YouTube to learn how to make one. The first wig Jane made was hideous. It was terrible. As bad as it looked, though, it still felt better than her actual hair. She told herself, *You know what? It's not too bad. Let me just keep going.* Jane kept at it.

One day, while Jane was working in the shoe store, a customer told her about going through chemotherapy and complained that her hair was falling out.

Jane said, "You know you can get a wig, right? I have one on right now."

At this point, Jane had made about ten wigs. Although she still considered herself an amateur, her skills had improved significantly.

The customer stared at Jane, then blurted, "Can I buy that one off your head?"

Jane thought her customer must be joking. She responded playfully, "No."

The customer said, "You don't understand how desperate I am to get one." She offered Jane $1,000 for the wig, and Jane sold it to her.

Jane could not believe what had just happened. In a matter of minutes, not only had she helped her customer reclaim a sense of her own beauty: She had also made money! It was the best of both worlds.

That night, Jane told her husband, Ed, "You know what, I'm going to start making wigs."

Ed responded, "What? Like, how did you know?" Ed had been thinking the same thing. He was on board with his wife's business idea. He had witnessed the improvement of Jane's skill set and understood the retail value of the product from conversations the two had shared.

At first Jane made and sold wigs part-time. But within three months, she was making enough in one week to match her monthly salary at the shoe store.

At that point, Jane told herself, *Okay, that's it.* Jane left her job at the shoe store to fully dedicate herself to her new company, The Virgin Hair Fantasy. Jane's famous wig line, Perucas, had officially launched.

As is true for many owners of minority business enterprises (whom I will refer to in this book as MBEs[1]), Jane and Ed are super talented in their work and their revenue reflects the devotion of their fans.

The Virgin Hair Fantasy took off. In an effort to build the brand and continue to surprise and delight their customers, Jane and Ed reinvested their profits in their business. Though their revenue flourished as they grew their company, their personal income did not. Although they could see the numerous deposits they'd made on their bank statements, they continued to struggle financially and their business did not produce a return on investment (ROI) that matched their endless efforts. They realized that something was wrong. How could you do what you love, do it well, and have nothing to show for it?

As children, Jane and Ed had both experienced trauma around money. They had both witnessed their parents' success and wealth disappear without explanation. Neither of them understood how their families could have gone from having money to having none, seemingly overnight. As Jane and Ed dealt with their own successes and financial challenges, their childhoods began to haunt them. Their families had been

---

[1] I know that you, as the owner, founder, and/or leader of a minority business enterprise, have a full life above and beyond your enterprise and are not interchangeable with it by any means. However, for the sake of clarity and simplicity in this book, I refer to owners, founders, and leaders of minority business enterprises as "MBEs" and the businesses themselves as "minority business enterprises." "MBE" is a designation bestowed upon minority-owned businesses by the National Minority Supplier Development Council, and by various local municipality procurement programs.

unable to pass down sophisticated financial strategies. Like many MBEs, they had to take it upon themselves to figure out how to make their business wildly successful. They did not want to end up like their parents. They had their own children; they had to get it right.

Jane and Ed went on a mission to figure out how to be better with money. Ed became obsessed. He read books and searched online.

Then, one day, he stumbled upon the book *Profit First*[2] by Mike Michalowicz. As Ed read the book, he thought, *This book is amazing. It just makes sense.* In fact, it made a lot of sense. The Profit First system is based on the old envelope technique, in which people stashed money for different expenses in different envelopes. Ed had heard of this approach before. The key difference with Profit First is, just as the name suggests, you take your profit *first*. Rather than waiting for leftovers after everyone else is paid, you take what *you* need to run your life and grow your own wealth *before* you cover expenses.

Ed continued to read *Profit First*. In fact, he loved it so much, he bought two copies so that both he and Jane could listen to the books on their phones simultaneously. As Jane and Ed finished the book, they both realized that they wanted to implement the suggested steps. However, they still needed help to customize the techniques for their business. They searched for a Profit First Professional, someone who is trained in the Profit First system. And that's how I met Jane and Ed Harris.

---

[2] Mike Michalowicz, Profit First (New York, NY: Penguin Random House LLC, 2017).

When implementing Profit First for The Virgin Hair Fantasy, I helped Jane and Ed determine their end goals. Then we created action steps and key performance indicators (KPIs) that would detect changes in their company's performance while monitoring their success at the same time.

Within twelve months, Jane and Ed achieved their financial end goals. They now sleep peacefully at night. They have become their families' first-generation millionaires. Their business now produces profits and cash flow that allow them to leave a legacy to their children.

When I interviewed her for this book, Jane told me, "When we realized that we needed help, when we saw that not all of the pieces of the puzzle were matching up for us, that's when we started seeking help. Seeking help doesn't make you weak. It makes you strong. I feel like, as a small business owner, you wear so many hats. This is one hat that you definitely need to delegate because it's one of the hats that changes everything in your business. So, I think it's not something to handle later. No, you handle it first. *Profit first.*"

I have worked with countless entrepreneurs who, like Jane and Ed Harris, started a business they loved only to find that it became like the Wachowskis' 1999 movie *The Matrix*: a prison from which there was no escape. These entrepreneurs have a gambler's hope that is soon snuffed out by never-ending customer expectations, hard work, and too little to show for their sacrifice. But it doesn't have to be that way. Using the same methodology and techniques that I use with my clients, anyone can change the legacy they have inherited and become the first-generation financial success story in their family. This is regardless of their race, background, gender, or starting point.

Statistics are discouraging. They tell us that, as MBEs, we are hopelessly disadvantaged. I could share the stats here, but I don't want to give them space they don't deserve. I believe that the success stories of ethnic minority business owners tell a different story. We, as people of color, continue to defy the odds. We create success that statistics just cannot explain.

In this book, I will not only teach you how to implement Profit First in your own business. I will also share the stories of other MBEs who were able to achieve success in a variety of different industries. I'll reveal the unspoken secrets of successful non-minority-owned businesses, which represent the majority of my client base. And I will teach you the key things you need to know in order to create the wildly cash-positive, profitable minority business enterprise of your dreams.

Onward. Let's begin.

CHAPTER ONE

A Better Way

My parents made it easy for me to understand where I stood. "In America, if you are one-eighth Black, you are Black," my father warned me. "You will have to work twice as hard, and be twice as good, just to be seen as average."

I STARED DOWN AT MY brand-new, healthy, brown baby girl, Florence. She had fat, juicy thighs and pudgy little arms, and she slept all day without a care in the world. I felt so grateful for and proud of the moments I got to spend with her. As I picked sleepy Florence out of her comfy, warm crib, I couldn't help but wonder: *What am I going to do next?*

Florence was six weeks old at the time, and I was scheduled to go back to work in two weeks. The last thing I wanted was to spend another year doing repetitive work at another corporate job. When I dreamed of having babies, I never thought of leaving them alone for hours at a time in day care. I was committed to being present and cheering Florence on as she experienced the most precious moments of her life.

Although I was scheduled to resume my corporate job, I knew I was capable of doing something very different. I wanted to live each day like it mattered. Returning to the hustle and grind of the corporate world would mean settling for a life that was the opposite of what I really wanted. I wanted to live a life that required innovation. I wanted to help entrepreneurs build successful businesses that provide opportunities for others.

A half-Chinese, half-Black kid, I was required to work in the family business growing up. I started doing bookkeeping for my dad's accounting firm when I was fourteen. His clients were mostly Chinese restaurants, and I loved perusing their books and records. I loved monitoring their revenue trends and looked forward to uncovering the secrets of how they spent their money. When analyzing their records, I could quickly identify what was working and what was just a waste of time.

Holding Florence and thinking about my work experiences in childhood, I realized that I wanted to help small business owners in a way I never could while working at a corporate job. I wanted to help them make better business decisions and acquire better opportunities.

Even more importantly, I wanted to show Florence that we could do and accomplish anything we wanted in life. I wanted to show her that I could, that *she* could, that *anyone* could be anything they wanted to be in this world. I wanted to give Florence a new legacy of self-confidence. I wanted her to believe she could carry the torch as we continued to *change* our family legacy.

As is true for the leaders of many minority business enterprises, I was used to being the first in my family to do many things. I came from a lineage of Southern Black sharecroppers and witnessed the generational impacts of slavery, poverty, and disadvantage. I was obsessed with continuing to build and change my family legacy. My mother's mother had passed away when my mother was eight years old, leaving her and her siblings to navigate the world on their own. Being the first of my mother's direct descendants to graduate from college was just the start of my adventure. I had already pivoted our family legacy; Florence was not an orphan, I had a college education, and I was determined to use my talents to change the world of entrepreneurship.

Many of the minority business enterprise founders I've met have shared with me that they, too, dream of changing their family legacy. They have a vision of improving their communities and leaving their businesses as inheritances for their children. These MBEs are proud of their work, and see the impact they have made both within their families and on the world around them. Many of them are also the first in their families to embark on the journey of entrepreneurship, and many have gone on to build businesses greater than themselves.

In this same spirit, I decided to start my own business—to step out into the world of entrepreneurship! I founded Mariga CPA PLLC to make an impact—on my own family, on my fellow MBEs, and on the world.

At first, starting my own accounting firm was exciting. I would wait until Florence took her naps, which in the beginning were plenty. Then I would type away on my six-year-old, worn-down, original blue Dell Inspiron laptop. During my precious moments of silence, I researched how to start a new business, how to market a new business, how to incorporate a new business, and how to get customers. I researched tax software packages, ordered paper publications from the IRS website, and read for hours to update myself on the latest and greatest tax rulings. I purchased a $20-dollar-a-month website that only provided me with a single-page web presence, but this was certainly adequate and allowed me to proudly display my brand-new P.O. Box address and cell phone number. I was off to the races, off to entrepreneurship, and so very excited about my new adventure.

As the days went by, Florence—as most babies do—slept less and less. She wanted more interaction and more daytime play, so I worked at night researching new customers, new marketing strategies, and new tax laws. Soon I was working two jobs: raising Florence during the day and Mariga CPA PLLC at night.

My first year, I earned negative $2,000. My second year, I got my marketing together, visited mompreneur groups, gave a few speeches, joined the chamber of commerce, and grossed $64,079. My bottom-line take-home pay that year was $20,182. I could have made more at my corporate job.

My third year, I got a little bit more sophisticated. I realized that I really liked working with business clients and doing business taxation. That year, I grossed $108,967 and netted $33,915—still less than I'd made at my corporate job.

During this time, I worked with many business clients. Most were owners of minority business enterprises, and many of them were first-generation entrepreneurs. We were all hustling to acquire clients and build our businesses, working at odd hours of the night and dropping our prices to compete, and most of us had absolutely *nothing* to show for it.

I got a little more sophisticated with my marketing, hired a sales team, spent a whole lot of money and time creating "affordable" accounting packages, and gained a plethora of price-shopping clients. When I finally made it to the six-figure net income mark, I couldn't fully appreciate it because I had given up my life in exchange.

Coming from top-tier Big Four accounting firms, I was accustomed to working with teams of strong problem-solvers with valuable communication skills and stellar work ethics. However, inexperienced employees were all I could afford in my own business. I simply did not have the margins or financial resources to hire the employees that I really wanted without sacrificing further by giving myself another pay cut. To recruit and hire an experienced person like me, even a younger version, I would have to pay them out of my own salary. I suffered from a scarcity mindset, so I chose to keep my inexperienced team and continued to work twelve-hour days, often till eleven at night. And I continued to cover for and correct employee mistakes so that no client would ever receive subpar work.

Lying in bed with prescribed muscle relaxers, the harsh reality hit me that something had to change. Everything I had worked for up until this point was giving me absolutely everything I did not want. No time, no life, no happiness. By this time, Florence and her brother Emmanuel were being raised by a nanny. I hardly got to see my kids, I was no longer living my purpose, and I couldn't help but think in disgust, *What kind of mom am I, for my kids?* Something had to change.

There were weeks that I had to forgo my own payroll in order to pay my employees, and I was fed up with paying myself the leftovers and exchanging all of my talent and hard work for scraps! I was tired of working endlessly, covering mistakes made by inexperienced employees, and having nothing to show for it.

I thought back to the message my parents communicated to me as a child: "In America, if you are one-eighth Black, you are Black. You will have to work twice as hard, and be twice as good, just to be seen as average." I had experienced that truth during my education and in the corporate world, and now I was experiencing it as an entrepreneur. I couldn't take being overworked and underpaid in a business that was supposed to change all that. I caught myself thinking, *If I just got hit by a car, God would take me out of my misery*. I was suffering from entrepreneurial depression.

In her 2013 *Inc.* magazine article, "The Psychological Price of Entrepreneurship,"[3] Jessica Bruder explores the anxiety, depression, and too-frequent suicides that result from the roller-coaster highs and lows associated with entrepreneurship. These dark emotions compound due to the isolation caused by the lack

---

[3] Bruder, Jessica. "The Psychological Price of Entrepreneurship." Inc. magazine, September, 2013. https://www.inc.com/magazine/201309/jessica-bruder/psychological-price-of-entrepreneurship.html

of close and sizable entrepreneurial communities. And there is an overall lack of openness within these networks about the realities of the journey. Entrepreneurs, in the effort to protect their brand image, are left to wrestle with challenges in isolation. Without relatable companionship, entrepreneurs often feel alone and somewhat "off." MBEs, if you have experienced or are experiencing this darkness, you are not alone! The traits of successful entrepreneurs are rare, and the daily requirement of taking calculated risks while making hard decisions that impact the lives of others is a tremendous burden to carry alone.

The day I found the book *Profit First*, I could hardly get of bed. Nothing I did seemed worth anything. The knowledge that I could earn much more if I just went back to my corporate job haunted me daily. I was devastated by the fact that I had built a volume-based business, a business that allowed me no time, no experienced employees, and, ultimately, no happiness. My lower back consistently hurt, my chest ached, and I was miserable.

At the time, I was a member of an online community of business owners. One morning, in my lethargic state after another sleepless night, I decided to put out an SOS. I told the whole world exactly how miserable I really was. Explicitly, I detailed how I felt taken advantage of, how ceaselessly I worked, and how I always covered for my team's mistakes. I confessed how I really wanted to fire an employee but could not afford a better replacement, how I had given this team member chance after chance, and how I just wanted to walk away from it all before it killed me anyway.

An outpouring of advice from the entrepreneurship community came immediately: "Fire that employee." "Move on." "This is not worth it." "I have been there before." And, *"Profit First*—you gotta read it!"

Sometimes your soul just guides you to the next step in your life's adventure. Mine fixated on the comment, *"Profit First*—you gotta read it!" I didn't have time to read, so I immediately ordered the audio version of the book. As I listened to Mike Michalowicz, I felt as though he had been watching me struggle, that his experiences mirrored my own. Finally, someone "got" me. Someone understood the misery of entrepreneurship. I had received validation from another being out there that I was normal, and I was not alone.

Listening to Mike, I discovered a name for my situation: "entrepreneurial poverty." Poverty of mind, money, time, and life.

I wanted out! I wanted change! I desperately needed to pivot and move in a different direction!

Sometimes life forces you to change. This was my moment. This was my wake-up call. If I was going to create the life I really wanted, and a business that would act as a conduit for my life's purpose, I could no longer allow myself to be shortchanged by my business and everyone else around me. I had to find a new way. I had to stop commoditizing my talent and claim my place of real value in this world.

So many of the MBEs I met that year shared that they felt the same way. Even if we weren't saying it, we were cutting our prices and treating ourselves as if we needed to work twice as hard just to be seen as equal to our "white" counterparts in the market.

If we are to create the change that we want to see in our own families and within our communities, we must stop commoditizing the talents that we bring to the market. We must stop marginalizing our efforts. We must elevate our own self-worth, and, my friend, this starts with taking our profit first!

PUT YOURSELF AND YOUR PROFIT FIRST

I WAS ALWAYS ONE OF the best students in school. When I graduated from Ohio State University, I joined Arthur Andersen, the prestigious accounting firm in Chicago. I worked with large, blue chip clients and learned complicated accounting principles, equations, and theories, but none of this was practical for running a small business.

For example, cash flow statements not only took additional time to properly prepare (the QuickBooks printout is not good enough, guys), but my small business accounting clients paying $200 a month did not value them. They did not have time to review them, and God forbid I ask them to pay more for the service. Even if they did receive and look at statements of cash flows, it would be likely be way too late for most of them to make use of the statements by the time they did. Besides, who cares what you did a year ago? "What should I do today?" That is the question for every entrepreneur! It doesn't matter if you were a good student, or struggle to understand financial statements. Nothing in academia or corporate accounting is useful for a small business entrepreneur.

Profit First, on the other hand, is a useful and practical system. The heart of it is in the words themselves: Profit. First. That phrase alone was a game-changer for me and, later, my clients.

As a small business owner, profit is yours and yours alone, and taking it first is the name of the game. After all, why be in business if you are not going to reap the rewards? That is exactly what the small business community needs to hear!

For decades, personal finance expert and radio talk show host Dave Ramsey has talked about the concept of paying yourself first on the personal level. For the average person, this means paying into your savings account and funding your retirement. Profit First takes it to the next level, and it is absolutely amazing! It is the proverbial chicken-before-the-egg concept. If you cannot pay yourself from your business, you will have no savings, much less any money left over for retirement.

Dave Ramsey's Financial Peace course teaches households to place cash in envelopes based upon their designated purposes. This allows the household to limit its spending with intention. In Profit First, which is designed for businesses, you start bank accounts instead of using Dave Ramsey's envelopes. A lot of bank accounts. These bank accounts act as envelopes. I use these bank accounts to appropriate money, and I use these bank accounts to establish my intentions. Each bank account has a designated purpose and restricts my spending. These bank accounts now ensure my profitability, because before I put any funds into an expense bank account, I take my profit first. It all makes complete sense!

In Profit First, all revenue is collected within a single bank account, the Income Account. Twice a month, we transfer money from the Income Account to several other bank accounts based upon pre-designated percentages. We transfer money to our Profit Account to ensure profits. We transfer money to our Tax Account to save for tax time. We transfer money to our Owner's Compensation (Owner's Comp) Account to ensure that we are always paid a fair salary. Finally, what is left over is transferred to the Operating Expense (OPEX) Account. By implementing this cash management system, we can immediately determine what amounts go toward salary, tax reserves, and profit.

When I learned the Profit First system, I knew it would help me generate profits, manage cash flow, establish boundaries, and gain an intuitive sense of when things were just not going right. As I implemented Profit First, I felt as if a lifeline had been thrown to me. I began to break boundaries. A $100,000 salary became nothing. Now I wanted 50% of everything my business earned.

The best thing happened: My biggest competitor—and my biggest obstacle—became myself. Each week, I found myself besting my best. I refused to cut my prices and sacrifice quality just to compete against others in the market. Instead, I raced against myself. This shift in mindset helped me see that the sky was the limit in terms of what I could achieve. No more boundaries or ceilings—it was just me and my numerical transfer goal.

I began to pave my own way and examine my own value. I reviewed my clients list and set out on a mission to discover what my clients really wanted. I researched what my clients valued, and ultimately uncovered their true needs. I analyzed ways I could rise to the occasion to meet my clients' demands and, ultimately, how I could fill the gaps. My attention shifted to the various ways I could make my clients über-successful. Their great success was my goal because the only way I would be able to make my transfer percentages was by helping others succeed in accomplishing their own goals.

I loved Profit First from the beginning! And when Mike spoke about Profit First Professionals, his community of accountants, bookkeepers, and coaches, I confess: I would have paid anything to join. Not just because I honestly considered it an opportunity to help others, but also because I needed to save my own life. Profit First Professionals recruited a die-hard!

It was a marriage made in heaven. Profit First allowed me to get to a place in my career where, if I did not limit myself, I could go where no one else could.

MBEs, if you allow yourself to go beyond your limits, you will also move beyond the pack. Your competitors simply will not have the stamina and innovation to do what you do. Your competitors will not earn the profits that you make and, ultimately, they will not have the funding to go to the places you go. At some point, the only competition that exists will be the fight against yourself. This is what Profit First did for me.

In implementing Profit First, I learned to compete against yesterday's accomplishments and drive value in a way that I never had before. My owner's compensation and profit were my reward.

Unbeknownst to me, by taking my profit first, I also changed my family's legacy. I built a profitable business, generated cash flows for other new investments, and, from a lineage of orphaned children, became the first millionaire in my family.

MBE, by taking your profit first, you will do so too! You will be able to reinvest in new ventures. You will change your family legacy. As you do, write and tell me all about it: smariga@SusanneMariga.com.

THE TALE OF TWO ENTREPRENEURS

BY ALL APPEARANCES, MICHELLE IS a successful entrepreneur. The Houston business community admires her. She is the recipient of many national awards, and her company was top-listed as a rising minority business enterprise. Over the years, her various accolades have included an E10 Award, bestowed by her local Minority Supplier Development Council, and a Goldman Sachs 10,000 investment grant.

Michelle is a force to be reckoned with. She drives a nice luxury Mercedes, pictures of her beautiful family are plastered online on social media, and she even created a nonprofit organization dedicated to giving people of color opportunities that they would never have experienced otherwise.

Her business portfolio includes several seven-figure government contracts as well as contracts with large retailers. Did I mention that she is also absolutely gorgeous? In her photo on the cover of *Business Journal,* she looks beautiful, strong, and untouchable.

As a tax accountant, I saw a different side of Michelle. Her financial records were in shambles. She had a constant flow of new and incompetent internal staff each year. When she applied for new contracts, she became frustrated because she did not have her records together. Seven-figure government contract after seven-figure government contract drove devastating financial losses for Michelle. One of her clients subsidized the financial losses from other, poorly performing clients. These individual job losses limited Michelle's earnings to only a low six-figure salary each year, while she served multiple million-dollar contracts annually. In our years of working together, there were many times when I witnessed Michelle bring home a loss only to be financially supported by her husband, who is a mechanic.

Michelle has big dreams. She's smart, bright, beautiful, and charming. She grew up in a single-mother household and set out to change her legacy for her children. A U.S. Army veteran, Michelle is a hard worker. In fact, she is one of the hardest-working women I know—as evidenced by the emails she sends me at two a.m., asking random questions about strategy or for an update.

So why does Michelle remain small? Why is it that she has so many gifts but cannot seem to rise above her current situation, even after a decade of trying?

Theresa is a successful businesswoman. She runs a multi-seven-figure IT company. She has multiple six-figure contracts with small and midsize investment companies. She is brilliant, charming, and kind. Her take-home pay is well into the multi-six-figure range. She is the epitome of success: a small-town, local gal who lives a humble lifestyle, yet is a millionaire in her own right. Theresa is also a white woman.

What makes Theresa's results different than Michelle's?

Theresa and her sister inherited their business from their uncle. Interestingly, when the business was her uncle's, it never quite seemed to achieve the success that Theresa has experienced. This is because, once Theresa took the reins of the business, she enlisted the right help. Over time, Theresa let go the advisors put in place by her uncle and replaced them with innovative thought leaders. The advice of these thought leaders helped her bring her business to the next level.

Theresa removed herself from long-term physical leases and allowed herself to build her talented team virtually. By building a virtual team, Theresa was able to enlist the best and the brightest around the county. She is a generous woman. Although she is conscientious about her budget, she realizes that to recruit the best and the brightest you must respect people and pay people their worth. If a client chooses to work with her, it is because of the quality of talent that she brings to the table. The price paid is what is required, and commensurate with the value of the work that she provides.

Theresa is not afraid to walk away from the wrong opportunities because this frees up resources for the right opportunities. She is clear about what she wants in life and in business. She does not hesitate to make her desires and expectations known to those on her team.

Theresa invests her time obtaining quality education. She often listens to Mike Michalowicz's *Entrepreneurship Elevated* podcast and does not hesitate to hire advisors who can take her to the next level. When Theresa makes a purchase, she considers the return on investment (ROI). She is highly dedicated to delivering the quality she promises.

What is the difference between Michelle and Theresa? One obvious disparity is that Theresa is a second-generation entrepreneur. She inherited a business that was already successful. Her uncle not only passed down industry know-how, he also gifted her with a pre-existing client list, stable relationships, and a board of advisors. More importantly, he gifted her with the strategy, thought processes, and tools needed to succeed. Theresa was smart enough to identify when she outgrew her board, and bravely embraced the new thought leadership that was required to take her company to the next level.

Theresa, like Michelle, is a visionary. The only difference in their approach is that Theresa does not look at life through a lens of scarcity, but rather through a lens of opportunity. She values people and what they bring to the table and is willing to compensate them accordingly because she knows that good people, "A" players, can always get an opportunity elsewhere and earn more. Theresa wants to be an employer of "choice." She wants "A" players to want to work for her. As a result, she offers health insurance, 401(k) plans, and a remote working environment; she gives her "A" players exactly what they want. In exchange, Theresa expects "A" players to perform as "A" players and drive the company forward.

Michelle's management levels are filled with family members. She has continuously put people into positions who are not qualified to do the work because she believes there are budget limitations that demand it. Michelle has a soft heart. She feels that she is an average gal, *blessed* with amazing opportunities. She truly believes that if you gift people with opportunity, they will rise to the occasion. Unfortunately, this has never proved true for her.

Although Michelle's team appreciates the opportunities she has given them, the confidence she has in them, and the pay increases she provides them, they rarely do the work that really allows them to shine. The staff really does work "hard" for Michelle, but they are not operating in their "zone of genius."[4] They are constantly swimming against the tide and are unable to intuitively excel. Even though they are working hard and putting in the hours, they are never able to achieve what Theresa's team achieves.

Michelle is haunted by the need to help her community and her family, and it comes at the expense of limited opportunities to propel her own success forward.

What would happen if Michelle became a little bit more like Theresa?

What would happen if Michelle unbound herself from societal expectations, embraced less tolerance for incompetence, hired "A" players for positions where they would naturally excel—and provided an environment in which they could do so—and charged her worth? What amazing success could she achieve?

Michelle wants nothing less than to achieve a level of success that she can be proud of. She wants to create a legacy for her

---

[4] Gay Hendricks, The Big Leap: Conquer Your Hidden Fear and Take Life to the Next Level (San Francisco, CA: HarperOne, 2010).

family. She dreams of financial stability. In order to attain this, Michelle first needs to start acting her worth.

WE ARE THE STORIES WE TELL OURSELVES

Fellow MBE: When I first began to write this book, I was tempted to fill it with statistics. Statistics related to how minority-owned businesses compare to non-minority-owned businesses. How Black-owned businesses compare to white-owned businesses. How educational systems differ depending on which neighborhood you live in. In fact, there are plenty of stats, stories, and theories that support the argument that we, as MBEs, are truly fighting an uphill battle. The sad impact of the statistics is that many MBEs will take this information as destiny. Some will accept it as truth. As a result, some will never take the next steps to pursue their dreams.

When I was conducting interviews for this book, one of the questions that I asked each entrepreneur of color was, "What has been your biggest challenge in starting and scaling your business?" I expected at least one or two people to say that it was being accepted in a room full of people who just did not look like them. To my surprise, no one said that. These brilliant entrepreneurs spoke of time management, understanding their financials, and implementing plans as a result of data. Some mentioned people management and just trusting in their own unique spark. No one once mentioned that their hindrance was the color of their skin.

Although my father meant well when he told me, "You will have to work twice as hard, and be twice as good, just to be seen as average," I took it to mean that I was "less than." He was insinuating that for me to earn a place in this world, to be accepted—heck, just to leave the neighborhood where I grew up—I would have to be better than anyone I ever came across.

Now, I don't think my father understood the psychological impact of his words. He just wanted me to have a better life than the one he had known. He just wanted me to rise and accomplish all of the things he never had the opportunity to do. His message, though, taught me that no matter what I did, no matter how hard I worked, I would just never be good enough. So I worked. I overcompensated and I became the best. I passed my Certified Public Accountant (CPA) examination on the first try. I told myself it was something I had to do. I did not realize that, in 1999, this was something only 4% of applicants in the country were able to do.

When you think that you are unworthy, no matter how hard you try, no matter how much you accomplish, nothing will ever make you good enough. Nothing you achieve will ever allow you to accept that you belong, that you are worthy enough to take a seat at the table.

Now, MBE, don't get me wrong—we do have to be the best in our fields. Any business that truly rises to the top must bring an offering that is in demand. Quality attracts demand like nothing else. Who wants to go where we know we will get shoddy work? Anyone who tells you otherwise is not looking out for your best interests. You have to be the best in your field to succeed in entrepreneurship.

However, being twice as good does not make you average. Being twice as good makes you *excellent*. When I look at leaders like General Colin Powell, Dr. Condoleezza Rice, Dr. Benjamin Carson, or Oprah Winfrey, I see heroes who are nowhere near the average. Heroes who have not only worked twice as hard, but have earned the respect of people of all races because of their brilliance in thought leadership. Each one of these heroes is from a very different background.

MBE: Working twice as hard and being twice as smart does not make you "average" in anyone's eyes. It makes you *excellent*. When you bring your talent to market in a way that changes people's lives, they will listen to you. This is regardless of your skin color and socioeconomic background. MBE: Be *excellent*. And, because you are excellent, do not accept the leftovers. Take your profit first. Take your pay first. Build a business that truly supports you, your vision, and your legacy.

Because you have come to where you are today, because you have mustered the bravery required to pursue entrepreneurship, I have no doubt that you also have everything it takes to build the business of your dreams. No matter whether you have been a "Michelle," a "Theresa," or a "Susanne," your past does not dictate how far you will go. The actions you take today and the choices you make each day thereafter determine your future. You can change your business. You can change your life. You can change your legacy.

Embracing Profit First is the beginning of acting your worth! Let's get started with giving you the know-how and tools to run a cash flow-positive, wildly profitable business so you can create a legacy of which you will be proud.

CHAPTER TWO

Take Your Profit First

DURING MY FIRST QUARTER IN business school at Ohio State University, I learned the traditional accounting equation:

$$Revenue - Expenses = Profit$$

We were asked to memorize this equation. We were tested on this equation. We were even challenged to algebraically solve for missing components using this equation. As my studies continued, I gained more knowledge of financial statements. I learned how to complete a Statement of Cash Flows, how to create a Management Discussion and Analysis (MD&A), how to roll forward a statement of equity, and, finally, how to create a Securities and Exchange Commission (SEC)-worthy, Generally Accepted Accounting Principles (GAAP) set of financial statements.

Later, I used my academic GAAP know-how during my first job out of college with Big Four accounting firm Arthur Andersen, LLP. There, I created real SEC-level financial statements.

Although my bound reports were beautiful and colorful, no one besides other accountants could appreciate them. I suspect that only accountants really understand them! When I present these statements to my small business clients in meetings, they swear that the documents are great and super helpful. However, I suspect that my beautiful, illustrated financial statements just end up in locked filing cabinets, never to be opened again. I know this because whenever these same clients apply for a bank mortgage or a minority business enterprise certification, they request another copy of the same reports. They let me know that they have (conveniently) misplaced the originals and can no longer locate them. Hmmm.

Most business owners should use their financials to manage cash activity in their businesses. However, there are two main problems associated with fancy financial statements prepared using GAAP. First, financial statements are views of the aftermath of business activity. They only show what happened in the past, which, in many cases, may no longer be relevant. The second reason is that most small business owners cannot afford to have an in-house accounting department. So, the timing of statement completion by external accountants versus when the activity occurred is often so far removed that, by the time this information is received, it is no longer useful. This leaves business owners guessing in real time as to what they should do next. They end up relying on intuition and, frankly, make decisions based upon their current bank balances.

Now don't get me wrong: There is a place for solid financial statements. Every business should have them. They are useful for deep-diving into line items, for seeing exactly where money is spent, for evaluating gross margins, and for uncovering inefficiencies that must be resolved to take the business to the next level.

However, you still need a system for the everyday cash management of the business. For most business owners, that system is eyeballing the bank account. We call this bank account accounting!

Bank account accounting is how most business owners make spending decisions. For example, when an exciting new piece of technology or software comes out, most small business owners will simply check their bank account balance to determine whether they should buy it. The owner will say either, "Yes, we have the funds; let's do this," or, "Well, maybe not today."

When payroll time rolls around, most small business owners will check the bank account balance and either sigh in relief or panic over how they will get more funding before it's time to make another payment.

That bank balance will have business owners questioning whether they should apply for a new line of credit, hire another team member, or fret that layoffs are just around the corner. Bank balance accounting is how many small business owners manage their day-to-day finances.

Parkinson's Law tells us that demand for a resource increases proportionally to its supply. Human beings are rather efficient. When there is plenty of a particular resource available, we use it in abundance. Most of us don't think for a second about it. In a world of plenty, there is no scarcity and no notion that something may run out; it will always be available tomorrow.

I love Mike Michalowicz's example in *Profit First*. He talks about a tube of toothpaste. When the tube is new, there is plenty of toothpaste. Whether you use a lot or a little it doesn't matter. It might annoy you a bit when your spouse squeezes the tube from the middle, but that is irrelevant. You use how much you use. If a little of it spills into the sink or drops on the floor, who cares? You simply wipe up the mess, toss it, and squeeze out some more.

As the toothpaste runs out, you intentionally squeeze the tube from the end to make sure you get maximum use from the resource. You begin to wonder: *Gosh, when am I going to be able to get to the drugstore again?* As each day passes and the tube empties, you use smaller and smaller dabs. Finally, the dab that comes out covers less than a quarter of the toothbrush head. Then you panic. You drop by the store, and the cycle begins again.

When the COVID-19 pandemic began, many people over-bought at the grocery store because they worried that products like soap, hand sanitizer, and toilet paper might soon be in short supply. They were living in a world of scarcity. Just a few months before, they were living like it was the Roaring Twenties! Our stock market was the highest it had ever been. Unemployment was low. For many people, money was plentiful. They were living Parkinson's Law.

In December, 2019, my business clients asked me questions like, "Should I buy that new truck for the business? If I buy that new truck, I might be able to take an IRC (Internal Revenue Code) § 179 write-off. This could be useful for taxes. Plus, this would allow me to put one more guy on the road to make sales and service our customers." Or, "Susanne, we are elbow-to-elbow in our office space right now. If we add any more people, we are going to have to have them sit out in the hallway. There is a space for lease down the street from us. It's a bit bigger than what we need, but I really think we can grow into it. It's a little more expensive than what we're paying now. A bit of a stretch for us, but I really think we will grow to fully occupy it."

However, during the pandemic, they're asking very different questions. "Susanne, what expenses can I cut so that we can make it through this?" "Which employees can I keep?" "How should I let my employees go?" "Are there grants available?" "If I take Paycheck Protection Program (PPP) money and use it to cover my payroll for eight weeks, what happens if I need to let my employees go after this?" My entrepreneurs are currently living in fear. They are living in scarcity mode.

As human beings, we are biologically and psychologically wired to build businesses that fail. This is part of the problem with GAAP and the overall approach to accounting. When we use the traditional "Revenue – Expenses = Profit" accounting equation, we teach accountants and business owners to focus on growing revenue. Concentrate on scaling. Whatever you do, make sure you are increasing sales. If it allows you to sell more, discount your prices. Here, we erroneously imply that if you focus on sales, undercut your prices, and accept every client, you will gain market share and surely make up for losses in volume.

Many of my peers tell business owners that if they stay responsible, pay all of their expenses, pay off their debt (better yet, avoid getting into debt in the first place) and sell their butts off, then naturally, just naturally, profit will follow.

Unfortunately, the reality is that profit never really follows in the volume we want. In fact, when we focus on sales, focus on revenue, and focus on paying our expenses, profit is usually just a measly by-product. Most of us entrepreneurs usually find out at the end of the year, when our accountants finally get around to completing our tax returns, that our profits aren't much to get excited about. It is not until we get intentional about our outcomes that we can begin aligning our actions to create the results we want.

In Profit First, we alter the accounting equation. Instead of the traditional equation,

$$Revenue - Expenses = Profit,$$

We use the Profit First equation:

$$Revenue - Profit = Expenses.$$

We prioritize profit. We literally take our profit first!

In Profit First, we work with our natural biological and physiological makeup. We own up to Parkinson's Law. Rather than operate from a scarcity mindset, we create an *illusion* of scarcity. We do this via the use of bank accounts.

Let's use the example of dieting illustrated by Mike Michalowicz in *Profit First*.

One of the first things we are taught when we go on a diet is the significance of portion size. (By the way, I feel like I have tried it all, and the only thing that works is eating less.) When learning about portion size, you hold up your fist; its size represents the size of a cup. Using your fist as a guide, you then determine portion sizes for your meat, carbohydrates, and vegetables.

I *love* the Golden Corral restaurant. (No gift certificates, please. Well, maybe, if you *must*.) It must resemble some part of heaven. So many plates, so many options—a life of plenty. The problem is, who can eat just one plate at Golden Corral? You must have a plate for a salad, a plate for the main course, a plate for dessert, and, who knows, maybe a plate for seconds.

But as lovely as I find Golden Corral—as tasty, as dream-worthy as it is—I have never left Golden Corral feeling proud of myself. In fact, I usually feel just the opposite. I feel bloated, tired, and disgusted, and often end up sleeping the afternoon away as I detox from all the unhealthy choices I have made.

It is not Golden Corral's fault. They are simply delivering on their promise of providing unlimited food-choice possibilities. And it is not my fault because I am simply behaving in the way I was designed to do. My body, my mind, and my mouth are simply following Parkinson's Law. Food is plentiful, so I am eating as if there is plenty. And when I tell myself, *I will not and should not ever do this again,* my mind innately acts as though I'm enjoying my last meal ever at the almighty, great Golden Corral: I must feast in celebration!

On the other hand, at an hors d'oeuvre dinner, I am trying my best to look good in front of my colleagues. We are dressed in our fancy suits and attire (which, by the way, are always a little tight on me). The last thing I want is to be viewed as a glutton, with my suit buttons popping off in a middle of a conversation. So, at this hors d'oeuvre dinner, I will naturally eat less. I will eat daintily. I will eat politely. I will not fill my plate. In fact, I bet my plate will actually be smaller. But regardless of plate size, my subconscious mind will feel comfort when the plate is full; when my plate is empty, I will feel as though have eaten enough. Instead of focusing on the food, I will focus on the conversation. The temptation to feast won't be there because I am an introvert. I hate to attract attention. Nothing attracts attention like the guy pigging out at the hors d'oeuvre bar. I actually dread these events. I don't want to return, ever. As a result, I will naturally eat less. I will make better decisions. I will leave my social event feeling proud of myself. At the same time, I will feel satisfied.

MODUS OPERANDI – PROFIT FIRST

IN PROFIT FIRST, WE CREATE the same illusion of scarcity. Instead of using plates, we use bank accounts. Our modus operandi is very similar to Dave Ramsey's Financial Peace envelope system, which I mentioned in Chapter 1. In Ramsey's system, money is placed in each envelope based upon its designated purpose (rent, grocery, savings, etc.). In Profit First, bank accounts are set up according to the money's designated purpose. This purpose is clearly delineated so that you as an entrepreneur know and understand it.

In Profit First, we set up five basic bank accounts.

BANK ACCOUNT 1: INCOME ACCOUNT

THE INCOME ACCOUNT IS USUALLY a checking account because of the transfer activity that will occur in this account. We recommend that you use a checking account for your Income Account, since the transfers out will usually exceed the legal limit allowed to maintain a free savings account.

The Income Account is used to collect all customer payments made to you in compensation for the goods and services that you provide. Literally all revenue that you earn is deposited into this account. Every single dime! Eyeballing this Income Account will show you your monthly cash revenue.

Then, on the 10th and 25th of the month, you will transfer the money that has accumulated in the Income Account to the appropriate bank accounts based upon their designated purposes. We refer to this activity as target allocation percentage (TAP) transfers. I recommend you do this twice a month for two reasons:

1. Twice-monthly transfers allow you to establish a habit and a rhythm. Once they are established, habits are difficult to break.

2. When you conduct transfers only twice a month and pay bills only twice a month, you will avoid becoming inundated with having to pay bills every single day. And because your bills will be paid at set intervals, you'll be

able to see what expenses you actually incur. This will force you to prioritize your expenses and make any necessary adjustments to create the healthy business that you deserve.

In Chapter 3, I will go into more detail regarding TAPs. I will also discuss how you can determine the percentages for each account that make the most sense for you and your business.

BANK ACCOUNT 2: PROFIT ACCOUNT

As you've already learned, the core of this system involves taking your profit first, so that is the first account to which you'll transfer funds from your Income Account. The Profit Account is typically set up as a savings account. Transfer money from the Income Account to the Profit Account twice a month.

When starting Profit First, I encourage you to consider making slow, gradual changes. Start with transferring a 1% allocation of all collections from the Income Account into the Profit Account. At any moment, you will be able to eyeball this account to determine how profitable your company has been for the quarter.

BANK ACCOUNT 3: OWNER'S COMPENSATION (OWNER'S COMP) ACCOUNT

The Owner's Compensation Account is also a savings account. This bank account will be used to collect and appropriate your owner's compensation. Yes, you must have this account. You *must* pay yourself.

This is non-negotiable! Too few business owners have a policy of compensating themselves first. When you don't have a policy regarding your own pay, you will rarely give yourself a fair shake. You must pay yourself, if only to establish a pattern that will enable you to hire your replacement.

Consider this the compensation that you earn for acting in the role of chief executive officer (CEO). When you step out of this role, you will have money set aside in your budget to pay your replacement. Sometimes, as CEOs, we don't get a chance to choose when we step down. Life happens. Unplanned events force us to make decisions that we would not make otherwise. When you budget for your salary and pay yourself, you create the opportunity to pay your replacement. This is a blessing if and when that replacement becomes a necessity.

BANK ACCOUNT 4: TAX ACCOUNT

THE TAX ACCOUNT IS A savings account reserved for your personal tax payments. Can you imagine not worrying about how much you will owe the IRS at the end of the year? When you use this system, you will have no cause for concern because you will already have saved for your tax obligations. Our minimum goal for the Tax Account is 15% of Real Revenue collections. (Don't worry, I will go into calculating Real Revenue in the next chapter.)

BANK ACCOUNT 5: OPEX (OPERATING EXPENSE) ACCOUNT

THE OPERATING EXPENSE ACCOUNT, WHICH we label OPEX, is a checking account. This account will be used to pay your expenses. Your rent, your utilities, your employee payroll, and any other expenses will come out of your OPEX account. Your expenses must be limited to the funds available in this account. The only money you have to spend on your business expenses will be the money in this account.

This bank account creates an illusion of scarcity. This is your small plate, your hors d'oeuvre plate. When your employee asks you to buy a new computer, or when you try to decide whether to invest in a new software subscription, this is the account you will need to review to ensure that you have the funds not only to cover your monthly expenses, but also any new ones. The OPEX Account holds all the money that you will have available to fund your operations.

BANK ACCOUNT 6: MATERIALS & SUBCONTRACTORS

FOR THOSE OF YOU WHO own manufacturing, retail, or construction companies that must purchase materials in order to produce revenue, I recommend you start another account called the Materials and Subcontractors (Mats and Subs) Account. This checking account will be used to fund the purchase of any materials for production and resale that you require to create sales in your business. It is similar to the traditional accounting line item, "cost of goods sold."

Please note that the Mats and Subs Account is not the same as a cost of goods sold account. However, it is similar. We will go into this in more detail in Chapter 8.

CREATING THESE SEPARATE BANK ACCOUNTS enables you to work with your natural psychological and biological makeup; what you are really creating is a mental and emotional illusion of scarcity.

You have taken the original accounting equation,

$$Revenue - Expense = Profit;$$

Struck a line through it,

$$\cancel{Revenue - Expense = Profit}$$

And inverted and reinvented it:

$$Revenue - Profit = Expense.$$

Now, you are taking your profit first!

PROFIT FIRST – A BEAUTIFUL FRAMEWORK FOR CASH MANAGEMENT SUCCESS

WHAT I LOVE ABOUT PROFIT First is that it creates a framework for you to be financially successful as a business owner. It literally works with your natural biological and psychological makeup to create boundaries for spending, financial controls that inhibit randomness and out-of-control spending habits. Profit First. It creates the perception of scarcity you need to make really hard decisions. This perception is necessary for the optimization of your business operations.

Profit First allows you, MBE, to take a home a real salary—a salary that will give you a sense of pride as it supports your family. You will gain a sense of comfort as you build up retained earnings. Your personal success will correlate with your business outcomes. And a high-revenue number will indicate a meaningful profit and owner's pay. You will be compensated for a job well done!

One thing I noticed when implementing Profit First within my own business was the anger I felt when I was unable to make a TAP transfer into my Profit or Owner's Comp Account. In those moments, I felt shorted. And it was during those moments that real and meaningful change was born. The frustration I experienced during those times of lack made me take a look at my internal operations. This led me to evaluate the positions on my team for efficiency and allowed me to take my company to the next level. I was able to have real conversations with myself regarding what was broken, what needed to be fixed, and what changes needed to occur for me to get back on target.

You too will get frustrated. There will be moments when you want to break down and sob. There will be times when you experience anger because there are just not enough resources available for you to do the things you want to do. These are the *beautiful* moments. These are the moments that drive change.

These are the events that will create efficiency. These are the opportunities that will help you build the business of your *dreams*. These are the life lessons that will mold you into who you *become*.

NEXT STEPS

Do not hesitate. Do not stop. Contact your banker today and open your minimum of five bank accounts:

- Income Account (checking)
- Profit Account (savings)
- Tax Account (savings)
- Owner's Compensation Account (savings)
- OPEX Account (checking)

Yes, your banker will look at you like you are crazy. Yes, you will have to consider the fees. However, time is crucial here. Think of the opportunities you will lose by delaying your start. The sooner you start, the more profit you'll make. And I will bet that your profit far exceeds the bank fees.

Many banks offer deals. For example, some will waive the fees if you start a savings account in addition to a checking account. Some banks will offer a minimum balance fee waiver if you open multiple accounts. But even if you don't have the minimum balance to start, you can work to get to that balance quickly. Don't get stuck in your head. Move quickly. Get those accounts started. Don't let a delay cause you a missed opportunity!

Next, commit to allocating 1% of your revenue into your Profit Account. Transfer this 1% into your Profit Account today. If you are already putting away at least 1% for profit, increase this by another 1%.

Look at you. Your year is already looking better than the one before! Welcome to Profit First!

After you have started your bank accounts and committed to a 1% profit allocation, let me know. Email me immediately at smariga@SusanneMariga.com. In the subject line, write: "I'm ALL in!" I read all my emails. When you let me know you are all in, I will start rooting for you!

CHAPTER THREE

Profit First: Target Allocation Percentages (TAPs)

IN CHAPTER 2, YOU LEARNED that Profit First allows you to be successful because it works with your natural psychological and biological makeup. This cash management system works by creating an illusion of scarcity.

By transferring funds to function-specific bank accounts, you create the small plate effect. When dieting, using small plates instead of large ones ensures that you will consume fewer calories. Your bank accounts act as smaller plates in that they limit available resources.

Using those function-specific bank accounts, you will naturally limit your business spending. Rather than looking at one main bank account—a very large plate—to determine if you have the funds to cover an expense, you'll check your OPEX (Operating Expense) Account. That OPEX Account is a smaller plate, so you'll naturally spend less than you would if you based financial decisions on your total revenue.

Immediately after funding your OPEX Account, you will feel sated. In such moments, it may seem as though your possibilities are limitless. However, as time goes on, your optimism may dissipate. Limited resources may make you feel as though there is never enough to cover your needs. You may find yourself searching frantically for new income sources, new opportunities, and new cost-cutting measures. This is exactly what we want to happen. It is during these moments of scarcity that you will reinvent who you are and the business you are building.

In this chapter, we will establish the amounts that you will habitually transfer to each designated bank account in order to build a financially healthy business. We will also create a bimonthly pattern for transferring the money into each account based upon its designated purpose.

THE RITUAL OF PROFIT ALLOCATION

YOU HAVE PROBABLY HEARD THE cliché: people are creatures of habit. Once we get into the groove of a particular behavior, we tend to repeat it. We often get to a point where we no longer recognize when we engage in these behaviors. These habits are rituals. They make us feel safe. They allow us to find our car keys in a hurry. They signal to our children when it is time to go to sleep.

Profit First works with our natural habits. It allows us to create a habit of paying bills on time and on particular dates. The dates that we pay our bills and make the required transfers are the 10th and 25th of the month. Paying on the 10th of the month covers bills that are due by midmonth. Paying on the 25th ensures that bills due by the end of the month, or the first of the month, are paid. If you invoice your clients on a monthly cycle via an automated clearing house (ACH), you may likely receive your funding on the first of the month. This will allow you to be fully funded by the time you make payments on the 10th of the month. If your business collects revenue throughout the month, as retail organizations and construction trades do, this payment system will also work for you. I do have some clients that choose different days instead of using the 10th and 25th; however, the core principle is the same.

Using the Profit First methodology, I want you to accumulate money in your Income Account throughout the month. Then, on the 10th and 25th of each month, make your target allocation percentage (TAP) transfers. Again, your TAP is a set percentage you allocate to each account. Money comes into your Income Account, and you disburse it according to your TAPs.

Right about now, you're probably wondering: "What amounts should I transfer on the 10th and 25th of the month?" Before we get into that, there is a key concept I want to explain: Real Revenue.

REAL REVENUE VS. TOTAL REVENUE

REAL REVENUE IS DIFFERENT FROM Total Revenue. Total Revenue is 100% of your sales collections. It is the amount listed on your income statement. To determine Real Revenue, you subtract the direct cost incurred in order to generate sales from your Total Revenue.

Examples of direct cost are the expenses incurred to manufacture your goods or services or to purchase the inventory you must have on hand in order to make sales. These expenses and inventory—the direct cost of production—are referred to in Profit First as your materials and subcontractors (mats and subs). We subtract the direct cost (mats and subs) from Total Revenue because, for the most part, you cannot fully control your direct cost. For example, if you do not purchase inventory for resale, you simply will not be able to make a sale. And if you are unwilling to purchase inventory at the market price, your vendor will simply find other willing buyers for their goods. If you are in the construction industry and unwilling to compensate your subcontractors for completion of the required work, your subcontractors will move on to the next prime contractor.

I want you to offer the best-quality services and products to your customers. Therefore, I want you to subtract your direct cost from your total revenue so that you can continue to reinvest in your business and maintain the cycle of revenue generation. Now don't get me wrong: There are ways to lower this direct cost. You can flex your negotiation powers and buy in volume. But for the most part, the cost to produce your goods and services is set by the market.

Going back to the business of Real Revenue: Simply put, Real Revenue is Total Revenue minus your materials and subcontractor costs (mats and subs).

Total Revenue – Mats and Subs = Real Revenue

Real Revenue is what is left over after you've paid for your required inventory, materials, and subcontractors. Real Revenue is the revenue truly available for discretionary spending within a business.

The choice to rent an office in a certain area and pay more or less for rent is yours. The decision to build an in-house team to support your operations or outsource your internal operations to free up your personal time is yours. You can choose to purchase name-brand rather than generic printer toner. You can choose to purchase vehicles with custom logo decals for your sales team instead of reimbursing them for mileage related to the use of their personal vehicles while on the job. Your Real Revenue is the amount of money that you have to spend on discretionary expenses. You must make choices accordingly to stay within those limits.

TARGET ALLOCATION PERCENTAGES

THE TABLE THAT FOLLOWS DEPICTS the results of a study performed by the Profit First Professionals Corporation and Mike Michalowicz. It indicates the common size percentages of a healthy company based upon the Real Revenue for each category.

Common size financial statements present each category as a percentage of total revenue. They allow us to compare companies of various sizes and industries to determine the percentage of each company's expenses in comparison to its total revenue. I love common size financial statements because they remove the bias of size or industry and allow us to make apples-to-apples comparisons of various companies.

	A	B	C	D	E	F
Real Revenue Range	$0 – $250K	$250K – $500K	$500K – $1M	$1M – $5M	$5M – $10M	$10M – $50M
Real Revenue	100%	100%	100%	100%	100%	100%
Profit	5%	10%	15%	10%	15%	20%
Owner's Comp	50%	35%	20%	10%	5%	0%
Tax	15%	15%	15%	15%	15%	15%
Operating Expenses	30%	40%	50%	65%	65%	65%

Figure 1: Target Allocation Percentages (TAPs)

The above table illustrates target allocation percentages in a healthy company. The columns represent the ideal percentages for each category: Profit, Owner's Comp, Tax, and OPEX. Note that the percentage allocation to the various bank accounts changes as a company grows. This change is particularly noticeable in the Owner's Comp category because the role of the owner evolves as the company begins to scale. In a small start-up company generating under $250,000 in Real Revenue, the owner does *everything*. The company is practically a one-person show. The owner is responsible for sales, for answering the phones, for fulfilling the orders, and for cleaning the bathroom! Naturally, owners who do all the work are compensated as if they are the sole employee. In the $250,000 Real Revenue category, owners receive 50% of all Real Revenue as compensation—$125,000.

As a company grows and scales over time, it relies more heavily on the power of the team. The owner is no longer responsible for completing the majority of the tasks by himself; they are now shared by various team members. When the company hits the $10,000,000 Real Revenue mark, the owner's individual salary is no longer a significant part of the company's Real Revenue. In fact, at $10,000,000, I might argue that the company no longer needs him for its day-to-day operations. The owner may engage in some public relations activity, but is now mainly an investor in a company that relies on team power.

As companies grow, profit allocation percentages also change. At Real Revenue of $250,000, for example, a company's profit allocation percentage is only 5%. But over time and with growth, it might gradually increase to up to 20%. Profit increases as the company grows because as Real Revenue grows, the owner is rewarded for the success of his team.

MBE, your TAPs are based on your Real Revenue category. When I work with my clients, I usually set a goal for them to work their way up to achieve the TAPs within a year to eighteen months. I find that when you make small adjustments each quarter, your likelihood for success increases exponentially.

Going back to the diet analogy: Just as you make incremental changes each week when you go on a diet, a similar approach to your finances will ultimately take you where you want to go. Small changes and adjustments accumulate. Over time, they will lead you to your goal.

THE PROFIT ASSESSMENT

NOW THAT YOU ARE BEGINNING to see where you want to be when using the Profit First system, let's assess where you are right now. When we map out an implementation plan in Profit First, we create a Profit Assessment. The Profit Assessment simply compares where you are today, in terms of common size percentages, against the TAPs for a healthy company.

Below is a sample Profit Assessment form.

	ACTUAL	PF%	PF$	THE BLEED	THE FIX
Top Line Revenue					
Material & Subs					
Real Revenue		100%			
Profit					
Owner's Comp					
Tax					
Operating Expenses					

Figure 2: Profit Assessment Form

1. In the Actual column, enter your Top Line Revenue for the last full twelve months. This is your total revenue from sales. This value should be the top line (or near it) on your profit and loss (P&L) statement. Other common labels for Top Line Revenue are Total Income, Total Sales, Revenue, Sales, and Net Sales.

2. If you are a manufacturer, retailer, or an entity with more than 25% of your sales derived from the resale or assembly of

inventory, put the cost of materials (not labor) for the last full twelve months in the Mats and Subs cell. This is *not*, I repeat, *not* the same as cost of goods sold. This is only for materials, and only if your materials cost 25% or more of your sales.

3. If subcontractors deliver the majority of your service, put the cost of the subcontractors for these twelve months in the Mats and Subs cell. (Subcontractors are people who work for you on a project basis, but have the ability to work autonomously and for others. They are not on your payroll; you pay them their project fee, and they handle their own taxes, benefits, etc.) In some cases, you will have both materials and subcontractor costs (think home construction). In that case, put the cumulative amount of these two costs in the cell. Remember to put only your materials and subcontractors cost here, not the cost of labor for your own employees.

4. If you are a service company and the majority of your services are provided by your employees (yourself included), put $0 in the Mats and Subs cell.

5. If your material or subcontractor costs are less than 25% of your Top Line Revenue, put $0 in the Mats and Subs cell. (We will account for these expenses in Operating Expenses in a little bit.)

6. If you are unsure of what to put in the Mats and Subs section, put $0. Do not overthink this. And do not use

this space to make nominal adjustments. The goal here is only to represent what your company really makes as revenue if the majority of cost is for materials, supplies, or subcontractors. Again, if you are even a wee bit unsure, put $0 in Mats and Subs. This will serve you better in the long run by making you more critical of your costs.

7. Now subtract your Mats and Subs number from your Top Line Revenue to calculate your Real Revenue, and plug that number into the Real Revenue cell. If you put $0 in the Mats and Subs section, just copy the Top Line Revenue number to the Real Revenue cell. The goal here is to get you to your Real Revenue number. This is the real money your company makes.

8. Now that we know your Real Revenue, let's start with profit first. Write down your actual profit from the last twelve months in the Profit cell. This is the cumulative profit you have sitting in the bank, or have distributed to yourself (and/or partners) as a bonus on top of—but not to supplement—your salary. If you think you have a profit, but it is not in the bank and was never distributed to you as a bonus, this means you don't really have a profit. (If it turns out you have less profit than you thought you would, it's likely you used it to pay down debt from previous years.)

9. In the Owner's Comp cell, put down how much you paid yourself (and any other owners of the business) these

past twelve months in regular payroll distributions, not profit distributions.

10. In the Tax cell, write how much tax your company has paid on your behalf. A critical point: This is not how much you have paid in taxes. This is how much money your company paid (or reimbursed you) in taxes. Tax is both the income tax of all the owners and any other corporate taxes. The likelihood that your company paid your taxes for you is very low. So, chances are, you will put a big fat $0 in this section, too. If your income taxes were deducted from your paycheck from the company, or you had to scratch together out-of-pocket cash to pay in at the end of the year, the company definitely did not pay your taxes and a big $0 goes in this cell.

11. In the Operating Expenses (OPEX) cell, add up the total expenses your business paid for the last twelve months— everything except your Profit, Owner's Comp, Tax, and any mats and subs that you have already accounted for. The expenses are listed on your income statement. Now, here is where people get confused. It's okay if the numbers don't match up perfectly. This is not accounting, and you don't need to reconcile to the penny. This system simply gets us to a ballpark figure of where we actually are, and then tells us where we need to start going. The goal is *not* to have perfect numbers; it is just to understand roughly where we stand now. And with that understanding, we can start working on a profit plan for our business. This is a starting point.

12. Double-check your work by adding up your Profit, Owner's Comp, Taxes, and OPEX to see if you get your Real Revenue number. If you don't get this number, something is off. Once you make sure all the numbers are as accurate as possible, adjust the OPEX number up or down to get the Real Revenue to balance. Now add your Real Revenue to the Mats and Subs figure and you should get the Top Line Revenue number. Make sure it all squares.

13. Next, enter the Profit First percentages in the TAP column based upon your Real Revenue Range. Use the percentages in Figure 1.

14. Copy the Real Revenue number from your Actual column to the PF $ Real Revenue cell. Then multiply that Real Revenue number by the TAP for each row and write down the number in the corresponding PF $ cell. Use this same process to calculate each cell in the PF $. These are your target PF $ amounts for each category.

15. In the Bleed column, take your Actual number and subtract the PF $ number. This is very likely to result in a negative number for Profit, Owner's Comp, OPEX, or all three. It is your "Bleed,: the amount you need to make up. Negative numbers mean you are bleeding money in these areas. Sometimes it is just one category with a problem, but in most cases, businesses are bleeding out in the Profit, Owner's Comp, and Tax Accounts and have a positive number (meaning excess) in OPEX. In other words, we are paying too little in Profit, Owner's Comp, and Taxes, and paying too much in OPEX.

16. The final column, Fix, will have no numbers, only the word "increase" or "decrease" in the cell for each category. If the number in the Bleed section is negative, put "increase" in the corresponding Fix cell because we need to increase our contribution to this category to correct the bleed. Conversely, if you have a positive number in the Bleed section, put *decrease* in the Fix cell, since this is a category where we need to spend less money.

Using this analysis, you can create a quarter-by-quarter road map of expense adjustments. This will provide you with a path to achieve your long-term goal or TAPs.

There is a sample completed Profit Assessment for a law firm listed on Figure 3.

	ACTUAL	PF%	PF$	THE BLEED	THE FIX
Top Line Revenue	$1,233,000				
Material & Subs	N/A				
Real Revenue	$1,233,000	100%	$1,233,000		
Profit	$5,000	10%	$123,000	($118,000)	Increase
Owner's Pay	$190,000	10%	$123,000	$67,000	Decrease
Tax	$95,000	15%	$184,950	($89,950)	Increase
Operating Expenses	$943,000	65%	$801,450	$141,550	Decrease

Figure 3: Completed Profit Assessment for Law Firm

I remember the initial disappointment I experienced when I first began to implement Profit First and realized the disparity between where I was and the Profit First target allocation percentage I desperately wanted to achieve. After witnessing entrepreneur after entrepreneur face that moment of realization, I now understand that it is one of the most critical moments in your path towards profitability. This realization and these emotions are the ones that you must embrace in order to create the business that you dream of owning in your near future.

PROFIT DISTRIBUTION

As I EXPLAINED ABOVE, EACH month, on the 10th and 25th, you transfer money from the Income Account into the Profit Account based upon the assigned target allocation percentage (TAP). This money accumulates, and, once the quarter ends, you celebrate by taking a profit distribution! This is very similar to a quarterly shareholder dividend that might be distributed in an U.S. Security Exchange Commission (SEC) publicly traded company. Now, as an owner, you get to take home *everything*. Well, not quite everything, but I will explain.

Part of the goal for Profit First is for you to build a self-sustaining, debt-free company. At the end of the quarter, you will take half of the money that has accumulated in the Profit Account and place it in another account called the Vault Account. We create this Vault Account because I want you to build *retained earnings*! I want you to be prepared for life's unexpected events. The next time you have to purchase equipment, I don't want you to be obliged to take out a loan or charge it on a credit card. I want you to have the money in retained earnings (the Vault) to make the investment. So, *today* we are starting a Vault Account. It will be funded with half of your profit until you have about six months of operating expenses saved in this account.

The other half of your accumulated profit becomes your quarterly distribution. That is, if you have no debt. (By the way, congratulations if you are in this position.) You now get a payout! WOOOOOHOOOO! This other half of your profit becomes your *mad* money. You can go out and buy that new piece of furniture, sign up for the *dream* family vacation, drop cash on that new car, or, even better, fund your retirement account. After my first profit distribution, I went out a bought a new piano and enrolled my kids in piano classes. I really wanted them to have the gift of music that I had growing up. WOOOOOOHOOOOO! You deserve this! I congratulate you!

OWNER'S COMPENSATION

Now, the Owner's Compensation Account is there to compensate you for your job well done! As an owner, you put a lot of energy, effort, love, and attention into your business. Not only do you deserve to be compensated, you *need* to be compensated. Heck, your family needs you to be compensated. I know a lot of owners struggle with this. Here's the truth: If you don't make your salary intentional, you will never pay yourself enough. I want you to be compensated in proportion to the performance of your business. This is why you *must* have a percentage allocated to Owner's Comp.

As I mentioned earlier, when the business is small, the owner is compensated at a rate of 50% of Real Revenue. Owners receive 50% of the Real Revenue because they do practically all the work.

One Saturday in 2013, I was sitting at my desk processing tax returns when my lower back went out. Boom! Just like that. I felt something snap and my back was useless for the month that followed.

That day had been a long one. I was exhausted, but April 15th was right around the corner. I just didn't have the luxury of taking a break. If I stopped processing tax returns, I would have had to file extensions, and I did not want to do that. Like so many of you, I decided to overextend myself to get it all done. When I overextended myself, I pushed my muscles beyond what they could handle. As a result of lengthening my workdays, I did not have time to exercise, so my muscles gradually weakened. Y'all have heard the saying "use it or lose it." That is exactly how your body works. In all my pushing and sacrificing to meet continual IRS deadlines, my body just decided to walk out on me. Have you ever experienced that phenomenon, when your mind is stronger than your body? This is exactly what happened to me on that Saturday in 2013.

The pain in my lower back was so agonizing that I could do nothing but lie in bed. After two days of intense pain, I ended up in my doctor's office. She prescribed muscle relaxers and 600 milligrams of ibuprofen. This was accompanied by strict instructions to rest and stay in bed.

This was a wake-up call for me. Although my mind was strong, my body had reached its limit. Pushing it any further would have resulted in permanent damage, a realization that hit me like a ton of bricks. I wished I had someone to back me up, an extra set of talented, smart hands that could pick up tax returns, make strategic decisions, guide clients, and just get it done. The problem was, I didn't charge enough and, as a result, I didn't have the margins to hire anybody with the experience the job required. So, taking pride in my reputation, I decided to absorb the lack. I worked the hours of two people. I got the job done.

The Owner's Comp is there, MBE, to compensate you for the work you do. It also serves as compensation for someone else in the event that you choose to or *must* step out of your business. The reality is that none of us will be able to work forever. *Every single one* of our bodies will stop functioning one day. Whether it be due to the flu, COVID-19, or something else, our bodies will give out. For some of us, this will happen unexpectedly. We must pay ourselves fairly, not only to build up our own personal savings, but also in the event that this occurs. We may unexpectedly need to pay someone else to complete the job that we thought only we can do. Pay your Owner's Comp, MBE!

TAXES

THE TAX ACCOUNT IN PROFIT First is set at 15%. This account is there for you to reserve for owner and business taxes at the end of the year. It is also there to shelter you from surprises. Prior to implementing Profit First with our clients, I remember the dread I would feel as a CPA when I informed business owners just how much they would owe at the end of the year. Yes, if you run a successful business and do not pay into the system during the year, you will *owe* at the end of the year.

Give your accountants a break, please! Stop making them feel like it's their fault. You know that if you are making money, you will owe taxes. It's part of life. Put on your big girl (or boy) pants and own your *success*. You did the work. You get to take the vacation. You bought that Bugatti. You drive on the freakin' roads: You pay the taxes.

In my *free* Profit First Master Class,[5] and later in this book, I discuss some high-net-worth tax planning strategies. These strategies are definitely useful for reducing your tax burden. However, at the end of the day, owning your success also means owning your responsibility. You can get into politics and try to change the system; you can protest their payment, but no matter where you go, *taxes will be part of your life.* So, save for taxes as you earn. Don't stress about taxes. Don't complain about them. Just create a reserve for them as you go. The more responsible you are up front, the more you intentionally put away for taxes, the less worried you will feel at the end of the year.

We use the schools. We use the roads. We drink the water. Let's not spend any more time complaining. Let's accept our fate and move on.

---

[5] If you'd like access to the free Profit First Master Class, visit https://www. SusanneMariga.com.

OPERATING EXPENSES

HOPEFULLY, YOU'VE ALREADY OPENED YOUR checking account for Operating Expenses (OPEX). This is the bank account you will use to fund all of your operating expenses. Review this account daily to see how much money is available for such expenses. Monitoring the cash balance in this account will drive you toward the right answers to questions like these: Do I have enough money to make additional investments? Should I upgrade my IT technology? Should I increase my spending on advertising?

As I mentioned earlier, this OPEX account will create an illusion of scarcity for you. When there is plenty of money in this account, you will celebrate. When the cash balance is low, you may feel heart palpitations. This is important because it indicates that you are working with your natural psychological and biological makeup. When money is plentiful, you will feel elation. When money is low, you will feel panic. This is the natural flow of your emotions in response to a world of plenty and a world of scarcity. Even more importantly, you will now be forced to decide how you will spend money on a daily basis. In a later chapter of this book, we will talk about budgeting, planning, and making decisions, but for now, you get the point.

THE CYCLE OF TRANSFERS

SO, ON THE 10TH AND the 25th of the month, I want you to transfer money that has been collected in the Income Account to the designated accounts:

- Profit
- Tax
- Owner's Comp
- Profit
- OPEX Account

Make transfers in accordance with the TAPs designated by your Real Revenue category. Now, I don't want to put your business in shock. Just as a dietician would never start by putting you on a zero-food-based diet, I encourage you to make slow and gradual changes to get to your target TAPs. You have heard the term "lifestyle adjustment." I want you to make a *business* lifestyle adjustment.

Start with a 1% profit allocation. You can do this! Just 1%. From there, you can increase the allocation each quarter. But for now, see what it feels like to have a 1% profit. (You'd be surprised by how many American businesses don't even have a 1% profit allocation.) If you ever get a chance, pull the Dun & Bradstreet report for your industry; you will discover the average profitability for that industry. And you will be surprised to find that, in most industries, the profitability rate is less than 2%. As an accountant, this has always *amazed* me. I always think back to the sly remark my dad made when he discovered that, after my first year of operations, my profit was actually a loss of $2,000. He told me, "It looks like you have been wasting a whole lot of time." Imagine how many businesses in America are just wasting a whole lot of time!

Over the next six quarters, I want you to increase your Profit, Tax, and Owner's Comp TAPs. As you increase your current allocation percentages (CAPs), you will decrease your operating expense percentage. Your CAPs are exactly that—where you are today. These are the percentages that you will adjust each quarter as you move closer to your target allocation percentages. Prepare yourself! You will have to make some hard decisions along the way. You may find that some of your loyal employees are not the most efficient beings out there. Some of the habits in which you've engaged will no longer serve you. You will have to make tough calls while implementing the Profit First methodology. However, you will be successful because you'll be doing it one step at a time.

Do you need a large office space anymore? Do you even need an office space? Can your team work remotely? What technologies exist that might allow you to deliver your product or service to market more efficiently and for less? How will you rise to the times? How will you do more with less? How will you cut and replace costs for greater efficiency? (I'll share more about how to cut expenses in Chapter 8.) Celebrate the wins! Celebrate the savings!

MBE, I know this seems like a lot, but don't get discouraged. When standing at the foot of the mountain, the hardest part is just getting started. Before you know it, you'll be halfway there! Be patient with yourself. The biggest opportunities lost are the ones that are never taken. Imagine what your life will look like when you have reached your TAPs. Imagine what will be out there for you when you achieve your financial goals. It's all waiting for you. Just take the first step. A journey only seems impossible at the beginning.

NEXT STEPS

1. Complete your Profit Assessment. Start with where you are today and create a plan to gradually reduce expenses each quarter until you reach your TAPs. For now, focus

   on the basic categories of Profit, Tax, Owner's Comp, OPEX, and Vault and the current allocation percentage (CAP) assigned to each category. *Do not get bogged down in the details at this point.* You will analyze your profit and loss each quarter for new cost savings.

2. Collect all revenue into a single checking account labeled "Income Account."

3. Each 10th and 25th of the month, perform bank transfers allocating all of these collections to Profit, Tax, Owner's Comp, and OPEX Accounts based upon the current allocation percentages (CAPs) denoted in your Profit Assessment.

4. Pay yourself on the 10th and 25th of each month from the Owner's Comp Account.

5. Pay your taxes associated with business earnings from the monies accumulated within the Tax Account. If you have a C Corporation, you will want to pay your corporate taxes from the Tax Account too. If you are a sole proprietor, single member LLC, or S Corporation, you will pay your

personal taxes from this Tax Account. You will do this by making a transfer to your personal account from the Tax Account in order to pay the IRS.

6. Quarterly, take half of what has been accumulated in the Profit Account and transfer this to a Vault Account to building retained earnings. The other half will be used to pay off your smallest debt. If you have no debt, congratulations! This half will be your quarterly bonus.

CHAPTER FOUR

Live Your Truth

I PULLED INTO THE COUNTRY club parking lot in my decade-old black Honda CRV. For the most part, it was reliable and could get me from point A to point B. However, it was not a pretty car. It had gray spots and a bit of rust, and had gotten scraped and dinged during a recent incident in a parking lot. These indentions were like my life; they proudly depicted that I had weathered a few of life's storms. I owned that CRV free and clear. Owning that car outright allowed me the freedom from debt I needed to start my new business without financial constraints.

I had been invited to attend a golf outing for the local minority business enterprise networking group. I loved that organization. It was full of committed business owners with big dreams. My MBE peers possessed charisma and energy. They were passionate about their products and services.

For this event, I had purchased a low-end set of clubs from a local sports retailer. I was eager to rub shoulders with the best.

When I pulled into the golf course, though, I thought, *This is not the place for me.* At the front of the parking lot, members in high-end luxury vehicles lined up for valet parking. Suddenly, my ten-year-old black Honda CRV seemed like an eyesore. I immediately made a hard right out of the main lot and hightailed it away from the fancy cars. I relocated to the rear parking lot where all the country club staff parked. There, my car fit just right. Some might say it actually looked like the luxury car of the group.

As I walked three miles in the scorching-hot Texas sun while golfing, I burned with embarrassment. I wondered just how these MBEs could afford luxury cars. What kind of businesses did they operate? What were they doing that I had missed? Maybe these movers and shakers were well beyond me. Perhaps I stuck out like a sore thumb, trying to hang at this country club.

Later that year, I became the accountant for many of these MBEs. Time and time again, they hemmed and hawed about having to pay taxes. Ted drove a gold Mercedes. He was put-together, professional, and always knew the latest mayor-so-and-so. However, Ted didn't like paying taxes. (I wouldn't either, if I hadn't been prepared to pay them.) As is true for many business owners, he neglected to reserve for his taxes and couldn't pay the bill when it came due.

I became accustomed to seeing tax returns that showed multi-six- or even seven-figure revenues for businesses with bottom-line earnings that were way out of proportion with their income. Meaning, I routinely came across net earnings of $100,000 or less for a *seven-figure* business. In fact, the average take-home for a seven-figure company was, sadly, around $50,000. The earned income credit (the credit the IRS gives you for just showing up to work, not being a success) became a regular calculation for me.

After preparing tax return after tax return, I shifted from wondering what these MBEs knew that I didn't to asking why they drove luxury vehicles when they really didn't even make enough money own their own homes. This was eye-opening. Suddenly, I became okay with my dented, rusted, ten-year-old Honda CRV. At least I owned my car and my home free and clear.

Many of the MBEs present at the annual golf event that day were there to rub shoulders with corporate diversity procurement personnel. (Most of whom, by the way, did not even drive luxury vehicles.) These MBEs hoped to get noticed so they would be awarded a corporate contract, which some of them did receive. But although some of their contracts allowed them to scale, many of the contracts were not so good. Some of them had margins so low that, although they covered the direct cost of labor and materials, there was nothing left for actual business operations. Scaling was difficult for these MBEs, and any hope of profit quickly vanished. Many of these contracts produced no profit and, due to the timing of when cost was incurred to provide services versus when payment was actually received, many MBEs found themselves unknowingly acting as short-term lenders to their corporate clients.

Despite their experiences, these MBEs continued to show up to the golf events, continued to attend the luncheons, and continued to maintain the hope that one day they would be afforded the opportunity to shine in front of corporate buyers.

Now don't get me wrong; networking organizations can be great. You can meet peers who deal with some of the same issues you face, and you can learn more about what the corporate procurement folks really want. And many of these organizations have scholarship opportunities and conferences. That said, at the end of the day, you have to realize that not all opportunities are good opportunities. More importantly, you have to live true to who you are, to your values, and to your reality.

One of the best growth moments for me personally was learning to appreciate my rusty, dented CRV. That car allowed me to start my business without the burden of debt, and I was immediately able to reap the rewards of my success. MBE, remember: You are in a race against yourself. Do not adopt other people's standards. What glitters is not always gold. What seems glorious may be accompanied by thorns. Appreciate where you are today. Stand in your truth, and be proud of your rusty, dented car if that means you are living a debt-free reality. By making wise decisions, and investing where it counts, you will one day become the envy of your peers!

YOU CAN'T BE THE CHEAPEST AND THE BEST

AS I SHARED IN CHAPTER 1, when I first started my business, I had just had my daughter, Florence. I figured I would play with my little girl, be a great mommy, have a couple of bookkeeping clients, do a few tax returns, and make half of what I use to make.

In my business plan, I determined to charge much less than my competitors and super-serve my clients. Naturally, over time, more business would follow. I doubt I'm the only one who thought like that. What I realized the hard way is that you cannot both exist as the lowest-cost provider and offer the highest-quality service. Trying to be both, I worked endless hours. I often stayed up through the night to meet my endless commitments, and I had nearly nothing to show for all of my effort.

As you already know, although strategically charging less than my competitors and undercutting my own prices brought me lots of clients, my margins were so low that I did not have enough revenue to hire quality help. My business couldn't grow. I was the only one who would work for free, and because I was the sole employee, I was working myself to death.

My experience is all too common. I see it with my clients, like Chris, every day. Chris is an amazing businessman who owned a staffing agency. He's smart and numbers-oriented, and he cares about his employees and his impact on the world. He's focused on creating generational wealth and leaving a new legacy to his family and children.

When I first met Chris, he could not get off the hamster wheel. He worked long hours, constantly writing up proposals and responding to requests for proposals (RFPs). He was a millionaire on paper, but he felt like he could never get anywhere. He had an army of employees and was known throughout his industry for his talented and diverse workforce. He was all over the news and social media and frequently gave speeches regarding the importance of creating opportunities for those who lacked them. He was seen as an asset to his community. And yet Chris had little to show for all this. In his multi-seven-figure organization, Chris barely made six figures a year. In fact, his six-figure salary was financed by debt. Each year, Chris ran a million-dollar loss.

I saw the truth because I was Chris's accountant. I saw his frustration. One day I confronted him about his insurmountable debt.

His eyes watered when I asked him about his endgame. In despair, he finally confessed, "I feel like I am drowning, and I just can't get out."

Chris had the multimillion-dollar contracts: contracts with governmental agencies and contracts with large corporations. He had the prestige. However, in exchange for the opportunity to play and gain this prestige, he had traded margins for volume. Chris initially believed that if he marked down his prices but sold more in volume, money would naturally start to flow in. He soon discovered that negative margins beget negative margins and, over time, accumulate into multimillion-dollar losses, excessive debt, and unpaid payroll taxes. Chris's only way out was to implement Profit First and prioritize his profit. He needed to say no to the "good opportunities," super-serve the great customers, and raise his prices.

There was no magic formula. No genie in the bottle. For Chris to get out of his situation, he simply had to embrace the practical, acknowledge his truth, and *change*.

Luckily for Chris, he had built a stellar reputation for being a high-quality service provider during his learning years. Although he had to let quite a few low-margin clients go, he was able to attract more high-quality *contracts*. At that point, he no longer had to struggle under the weight of bondage that resulted from super-serving low-margin contracts. This freed him and his staff, and allowed him the cash flow and resources to service his new, high-margin customers.

You can't succeed at being both the cheapest and best option. You just can't. Part of living in your truth is accepting this reality.

THE PARETO PRINCIPLE

THE PARETO PRINCIPLE TELLS US that 80% of our income will be generated by just 20% of our clients. This means that, statistically, we will spend 80% of our time, energy, thought, and resources on pursuits that produce just 20% of our results. The Pareto Principle predicts that we will waste a whole lot of time and money.

Before he implemented Profit First, Chris was so focused on landing large corporate and government contracts, applying to every request for proposal (RFP), and trying to figure out how he could make himself attractive to everyone that he found himself getting nowhere. Staffing agencies have very tight margins. I find it interesting when I see folks caught up in the allure of that industry because they are caught up in an illusion that they will make millions. When entering contracts to provide staffing services, the bill rate can seem generous. However, when one considers the payroll taxes and required overhead to bring the services to market, the margins are slim in most cases. Many are disappointed to find that staffing contracts produce an average profit of less than 6% of revenue. Chris started focusing on clients who produced a markup rate of 50% or higher. In his business, a markup of 55% generated a gross margin of 35%.

What would happen, MBE, if you spent your time and resources focusing on the 20% of your customers who produce 80% of your bottom line? What would happen if you focused your time, energy, thought, and effort only on work that generates gross margins of 80% or higher?

When I first started my company, I struggled with the thought of turning away business. I felt that if someone wanted to work with me, I had an obligation to help them out. Wasn't it a waste of God-given opportunity to turn away the money? Even if I had never done something before, I accepted the work. Of course, I believed—as my experience had taught me—that I could figure anything out! So, again and again, I told myself it wouldn't be an issue.

As a result, during my early years in business, I accepted every client and every project, and I did every job. The problem was, I was inefficient *because* I spent a whole lot of time figuring things out—studying how things should look, how they should work, and reverse-engineering final products. That's fine if you are in a single line of business where you invest your time, energy, and money to learn a repeatable task that you will use time and time again. Unfortunately, I was not doing that. I figured things out just to dabble in a whole lot of situations that I would never be in again. And although I gained new skills and sharpened my problem-solving acumen, I wasted a whole lot of time.

I would have been much more efficient if I had focused on my zone of genius. "Zone of genius" is a term coined by author Gay Hendricks, in his book *The Big Leap*,[6] that refers to your natural gifts and talents. When you limit your work to your zone of genius, you can achieve maximum effectiveness.

I once had an excellent conversation with a fellow accountant, Joseph Pancerella. He is a process genius. At the time, my business was still an all-inclusive, accountant-for-everyone-type firm, and we were struggling to implement effective marketing and lead generation.

Pancerella told me a story about a company known throughout the world as the best manufacturer of blue pants. When you purchase blue pants from this company, they are guaranteed to fit. The pants make you look like a million dollars—they curve where they are supposed to curve, the seams line up just the way they should, and the pockets land at just the right place on one's backside.

Not only do these pants look great and sell like the timeless classic they are, they are also extremely profitable for the Blue Pants Manufacturer to produce. This company has experienced employees who work with established patterns. Its suppliers are at its beck and call, and the raw materials required to make these blue pants are plentiful. Customers are always lined up for the next batch.

Now what if, one day, I call the Blue Pants Manufacturer and say, "Hey, I've been a loyal customer, but I have a very special project for you. You see, I have a special going on, and I need

---

[6] Gay Hendricks, The Big Leap: Conquer Your Hidden Fear and Take Life to the Next Level (San Francisco, CA: HarperOne, 2010).

pink polka-dot pants." Since I have been a loyal customer of the Blue Pants Manufacturer, they are innately loyal to me. They only want me to succeed. Obligingly, they accept my order.

The result is that, suddenly, the Blue Pants Manufacturer is no longer the best manufacturer of blue pants. They are no longer efficient or profitable, you see, because when the Blue Pants Manufacturer took my "special order" for pink polka-dot pants, it meant they had to rethread their looms. It meant they had to relay a new pattern and teach their employees how to line up polka-dot seams.

When I, the customer, receive my order of pink polka-dot pants, I note that it not only took longer for the Blue Pants Manufacturer to sew my pants; also, the seams don't always line up, which makes the polka-dot pattern look random. Worse, the pink polka-dot pants just don't quite fit the way they are supposed to. Sadly, because they accepted my special project, the Blue Pants Manufacturer is no longer profitable. They are no longer operating in their zone of genius.

The Pareto Principle teaches us that 20% of our customers will generate 80% of our bottom line. Imagine if you spent your time, effort, and talent on your zone of genius—the work that would allow you to produce 80% of your bottom of line. What would that do for your business?

Spend your time, energy, and effort only on the things that generate 80% of your bottom line. Allow someone else to specialize in pink polka-dot pants. Stick with what you know best, your zone of genius. Not all money is good money. Not all opportunities are great opportunities. Sometimes the wrong opportunities will cost you the right opportunities.

Know what you are good at, stick with it, and build on your genius.

NEXT STEPS

1. Determine which of your offerings are the most profitable. If you produce multiple service lines or products, create a profit and loss statement separating the activity for each service line and product. Which service or product line produces the greatest margins for you? Which service or product line eats away at the profits generated by others? Cut the lines of business that do not produce for you, or consider significantly raising your prices.

2. Prioritize task management. Do you already have a list of all the tasks you perform as a business owner? If not, now is the time to make one. Use the following Task Management List as a guide to help you label each task according to its level of priority. Within Figure 4, the infinity sign indicates a systematic process improvement. The smiley face improves your customers' overall experience. The dollar sign indicates that this is a revenue generation activity. If all three signs are selected this is a high priority activity. If none are selected, this task is not a priority. You will want to first tackle activities which improve your overall processes, positively impacts the customers' experience, and generates revenue for your business.

TYPE	PRIORITY	DEFINITION
$ ☺ ∞	1	Create a repeatable system that will make money in the next 60 days by serving a client (e.g. a website design that can be a template for many future clients' sites)
$ ☺	2	Generate revenue in the next 60 days from an existing client (e.g. a sales quote for an existing client)
$ ∞	3	Generate revenue from new clients and result in a repeatable system (e.g. a new product launch)
☺ ∞	4	Cater to clients and result in a repeatable system, but not generate money directly (e.g. implementing project management software)
$	5	Generate revenue within the next 60 days (e.g. a sales quote for a prospect)
☺	6	Serve an existing client, but won't directly result in revenue (e.g. modification to an existing contract at client's request)
∞	7	Create repeatable systems (e.g. form email responses to common questions)
(blank)	8	Though relevant and possibly important, won't generate revenue in the next 60 days, don't serve an existing client and won't create a repeatable system

Figure 4: Task Management List

3. Make a separate list of each of your customers, from highest to lowest in order of the amount of revenue they bring in. Place a smiley face next the customers you enjoy working with. Place a frowny face next to the customers who do not bring you joy. Analyze the profitability of each customer. If a customer is low on profitability and has a frowny face next to their name, cut the customer.

CHAPTER FIVE

Define Your Outcome

IN THE MIDST OF MY darkest days as an MBE, I decided to sign up for the MS 150, a two-day bike ride fundraiser in support of Multiple Sclerosis (MS) research and treatment that starts in Houston and ends in Austin. To me, the bike ride meant *freedom*. No one would bother me, no one would ask me repetitive questions, and, for at least a few moments, I would not have to solve the world's problems. It would be just me, my bike, and nothing but good ole nature.

When I started practicing for the race, building my stamina and endurance, I badly wanted to have a friend join me. We could raise money for a charity that helped others. On the fun side, we'd get to spend plenty of time together. And what human can ride for two days straight, practice weekly for hours, and not lose any weight? Win, win, win, right? I asked each of my friends if they would join me on the ride. Although I received a lot of compliments on my great endeavor and even some donations, no one accepted the challenge to ride.

I ended up joining a local bike club, where I met some great folks, none of whom looked like me. We started our practices as a group of strangers with nothing in common except for the love of road biking and a dedication to seeing each other finish our rides. We pushed each other, encouraged one another, and ultimately met the challenge of the MS 150.

The group gave me the role of "anchor," which meant that it was my job to make sure everyone finished the rides. It sounds like an honor, but they gave me that role because I was the slowest cyclist in the club. Being the anchor was something I was naturally good at. I truly care about people, and if someone new joined us, I made sure they too finished the ride.

The great thing about riding your bike and being the slowest in the pack is that you get to cruise past the trees, speed down the hills, and blast your music—and you have plenty of time to think. During our four- to six-hour training rides, I analyzed the events of my life and uncovered some of their true lessons and gifts. I was just about to turn forty, and my life was everything but what I wanted it to be. Although those around me saw my attempt at athleticism as a hero's journey, I understood it as a midlife crisis and a cry for help. Even though I was helping many with my fundraising efforts and improving my health, I was mostly doing it because I figured I had nothing to lose. I hardly saw my kids. I spent most of my time covering for my employees' mistakes, and, frankly, my dream of entrepreneurship had turned into an ironic nightmare. Though our end product was great, our greatness could only be attributed to the amount of time I spent cleaning up after everybody else. Coming home at eleven p.m. was not unusual for me, and I felt like a stranger in my own home and marriage.

Prior to the MS 150, I had not ridden my bike in almost eighteen years. But I found road biking fun, if a little dangerous.

When you are out on the road on your carbon bike, you are pretty vulnerable. Even outfitted with the best of helmets, when a car swipes you, it becomes a matter between you and God. However, the sheer exhilaration I experienced from having time alone, racing down hills while escaping a world that made demands on me every second of the day, was worth the risk.

The day of the race, I was eager to hit the road. The excitement of the unknown piqued my curiosity. The exhilaration of being amongst thousands of cyclists as we cruised uncharted terrain thrilled me. I envisioned hills to climb and, even more fun, steep slopes to descend. My many months of practice would now be tested. As my family looked on at the starting line, I knew that the last thing I ever wanted to do was disappoint them by not finishing the ride.

I was armed with my radio for entertainment, and enough snacks and water to make any camel content for the day. This was the moment I had dreamed about for months. And I looked forward to hours and hours of just me and my bike. Hours to think about the coming decade of my life, and every opportunity to test what I was really made of at this point.

Being alone for long stretches of time made me appreciate the fact that some of the greatest things we ever do in life are the things we have to do alone. Whether this is starting a business or starting a race, to accomplish the things that matter, we will most likely need to go it alone. Most people won't have the courage to come with us. Some will actually call us crazy for our audacity. Some will offer excuses. However, we should expect to work alone when we go after the things we really want in life.

You are the captain of your life. Only you can determine where you will go. Yes, there will be challenges—and hills along the way—but only you can choose to carry yourself to the finish line.

I have a photo of me crossing the finish line, that day of the race. Though it is not the most flattering picture, it makes me smile all the same. You see, I was thirty-nine years old when I decided to sign up for the ride, and not exactly in the best of shape in my life. Good photography depicts where you are physically, even if you have an entirely different mental image of yourself. Looking at the photo, I often laugh at the random, skinny, professional cyclist who was next to me as we crossed the finish line. Being at his side makes me look comical; I appear larger than life on my tiny carbon bike. But the fact remains: I made it. I finished the race that no one thought I would finish, and my family witnessed it.

Everyone's journey will be different. It's not about being the slowest, or about whether you are in the midst of the best or worst days of your life. It's about finishing the race in a way that makes you feel proud.

TAKE CONTROL OF YOUR THOUGHTS

WHILE I WAS GOING THROUGH my Profit First certification, I realized that I had to better understand human psychology in order to impact the lives of entrepreneurs and guide them toward the actions that produce desired results. So, I also gained my certification as a John Maxwell Team coach. During this coaching certification process, Christian Simpson shared an image of a stick figure with a rather large head and a pencil-thin body. The figure's head represented the mind, which consists of two major parts: a conscious mind and a subconscious mind.

The conscious mind controls one's thoughts, which, in turn, control actions, beliefs, and decisions. The subconscious mind controls one's feeling and emotions, and the chemical reactions that occur within the body as a result of those emotions. When human beings experience emotion, their brains' nerve endings fire, creating adrenaline and other hormonal responses along the neurons' synapses. These responses then radiate out into the body, fueling chemical reactions that lead to physical actions and, finally, results.

So, when my stick figure ponders good, positive, and powerful thoughts, it experiences feelings of excitement, hope, and optimism. These feelings move the stick figure to action, creating fulfilling moments of productivity that in turn release powerful, "happy" hormones like endorphins into its body. The endorphins influence my figure's body in such a way that it will move naturally toward those actions that allow it to accomplish the goals of its conscious mind.

In contrast, when the figure focuses on negativity and thoughts of fear and scarcity, the opposite occurs; it produces negative emotions in its subconscious mind. This then creates negative hormonal responses, such as stress and anxiety. Now, instead of feeling elated and excited, the figure will feel fearful, deflated, defeated, and tired; its body will behave in the same way.

MBE, choose your thoughts wisely. The thoughts you choose to entertain have the power to propel you forward or cause you to shrink back in fear.

I understand. Sometimes thoughts just happen. We sit through a day and thousands of thoughts flow through our mind. Thoughts of positivity, greatness, and next steps. Sometimes these are quickly followed by notions of loss, scarcity, and impending doom.

The truth is, we can choose the thoughts we allow our minds to dwell on. I love this Bible scripture in Philippians 4:8, NIV: "Whatever is pure, whatever is lovely, what is admirable—if anything is excellent or praiseworthy, think about such things." MBE, we have the *power* to choose the thoughts with which we fill our conscious mind. We also have the power to choose what we allow our subconscious mind to experience and dwell on. If we have the power to control our subconscious mind, we have the power to choose our bodies' reactions. Therefore, we have the power to predetermine our *results* and our *outcomes*. The mind is a powerful thing, MBE, and by choosing carefully, you can determine whether your outcomes are negative or positive.

WHAT DOES WINNING LOOK LIKE TO YOU?

I met Chris Oakley in the spring of 2016. He was working as a business coach at Dave Ramsey's Entreleadership. That was a tough year for my business. My eyes still well up with tears when I think of that period of my life. Nevertheless, I hope that we all get to experience these times, even though they are difficult, because they teach us our greatest lessons.

That spring, Chris Oakley posed an unusual question during a workshop seminar. He asked, "What does winning look like in your business?"

Although it was a simple question, it stopped me dead in my tracks. I had never thought about what winning looked like in my business before. I had never stopped to think about what success meant to me personally, or what my endgame might look like.

That question hit home like a brick flying at my face, and I was suddenly faced with the reality that I was just plain miserable. My goals for starting a business had not been fulfilled. I had ventured into entrepreneurship to be with my daughter, to have more time and more freedom. The only thing I experienced was watching the nightlight burn out as I wasted my life sitting at my desk.

It was not until the moment that I defined what winning looked like for me that I began to create the outcome I really wanted. Gaining clarity around my outcome allowed me to align my actions to achieve my long-term goals. MBE, you *must, must, must* define what winning looks like for *you*. The earlier you do it, the better. Heck, if you can do it before you even start your business, you *are* winning!

When I think about what winning looks like, I not only consider what I want for my business, but also what I want to experience in my personal life. How much time do I want to spend away from my business? What will I do with this time away? How much time do I want to take for vacation? How many days or hours do I really want to invest in my business each week? How many years do I really want to be involved in the operations of the business?

I also think of questions such as: What does retirement look like? How much money will I have then? Where will I live? What types of properties do I want to own? How will I fund my retirement? What do I want to leave to my children? What impact do I want to have on my community? What impact do I want to have on this *world*?

After I define what winning really looks like for me, I consider each goal and ask myself, am I currently on track for this? Is winning actually a reality today? If I am not winning, what is currently missing that is blocking me from experiencing my blessing? What item, although on track, is not quite there? If I am not winning today, if I am not accomplishing what I want for my business or my life, what do I need to put in place in order to win?

For example, if I am working really long hours in my business and I can't seem to stop, what is causing me to waste my life at the office? Is it that I don't have enough people working for me? Am I stretched too thin, trying to make payroll each week? Are the people who surround me able to support my vision? Do the people in my current team boost me? Are they pushing me toward the greater goal? Does my team have the right skill sets? More importantly, do they have the work ethic and dedication to do the jobs allotted to them? If my team possesses the dedication and all the right skill sets and ethics, what exactly *are* they missing?

MBE, you will have to dig deep here. Does your team member lack skills simply because they need a little more training or a few extra classes, or does the issue run deeper? Could it be that this team member is simply not a fit for the job? Is the job outside of this team member's zone of genius? Could the reality be that, no matter how many dollars you throw at them, no matter how much time, attention, and love you give them, they will never rise to the occasion because this job is just not what they were ever meant to do?

MBE, when you allow someone to operate outside of their zone of genius—when you allow someone to just keep a "job"— the power team you've dreamed of having cannot be. And if you don't build a team that allows you to win, you will always have to overcompensate by either doing the work yourself or burning your "A" players' candles at both ends, burning them out in the process.

MBE, what does winning look like in your business?

What would make your life a joy? What would make your heart skip a beat and make you shout to the world that you are happy? MBE, how do *you* spell H-A-P-P-Y?

Next, ask yourself: What must be true for that winning to occur? What is currently missing that, if it were present, would allow this winning to occur? What is currently *broken* that is not allowing you to achieve wins in your business? Prepare yourself; there may be many answers to that question.

I want you to write it all down: What is missing? What is broken? Make a long yet complete list.

Next, make a second list of what will help you address the challenges in your business. What must be true for winning to occur? What set of circumstances or talents must be present to allow winning to occur in your business? Don't hold back. This is not a five-second exercise. It will take some time.

Remember to also consider your thoughts. What shifts in your mindset need to be made in order for you to win?

If you have, as I once did, allowed setbacks to go on for a length of time, facing the truth on paper may bring you to the verge of tears. That is absolutely okay. Sometimes acknowledging the unfairness and naming the *pain* allows us to move forward to repair the damage.

MBE, after you have identified what winning looks like for you, what is missing, and what is broken, I want you to answer another question for me. What would it mean for you to win? What doors would this open for you? What would this winning allow you to experience? What would your life be like if you just allowed yourself to *win*?

Then, after you've made these lists, I want you to create action plans to address the items you listed as broken or missing. I want you to *win*!

In your action plan, list key milestones and key due dates. Then, monitor your plan weekly.

When I did this, I realized that the entire business revolved around me. All questions funneled back to me. When there was something broken, I was involved in fixing it. To create a decentralized thought leadership culture, I needed to shift the daily decision-making to the process owners. I needed to empower those involved in the day-to-day to make decisions. Now, I could not give this responsibility to just anybody. That would have been reckless. I had to ensure first that I had the right person on board for each position.

As we are in accounting services, a strong academic performance background was a must. But just having knowledge was not enough. Candidates needed to have the capacity to deduce reasonable and efficient solutions to day-to-day challenges. This required that we implement a way of measuring practical problem-solving ability as part of our hiring process. So, we created a test that our candidates needed to pass that included an everyday problem they might encounter. Although we did not expect them to solve the problem with 100% accuracy at the time of hiring (training is needed in most cases), we did look at how they approached and attempted to solve the problem at hand.

Once we hired candidates with the problem-solving capability the job demanded, we implemented a culture in which team members could no longer just hand off problems to be solved, but had to offer solutions instead. For our management level positions, we required up-front testing of project management capacity. Candidates that did not score above average or excellent were not considered. (By the way, using a numerical, unbiased score is a great way to rapidly sift through hundreds of applications.) Making these changes, though not always easy, was the best way for me to build a team of independent thought leaders with whom I am proud to be associated today.

Fellow MBE, when you define what winning looks like for you, dare to dream *big*! Dare to dream out of your comfort zone. Dare to dream out of the comfort zones of those around you. May your dreams outpace those of your family and friends. *You* are a trailblazer. *You* are the opportunity creator. *You* will carry the torch for our next generation! Dream *big*! You are our gen-one!

MBE, it must be said that, along the way, you will encounter naysayers. There will be people who tell you that you are crazy. They will try to convince you that this undertaking is just not in your zone of genius. Don't listen to them. Rise above their negativity.

Before Steve Jobs thought of the iPhone, there was no iPhone. Today, iPhones sell like a fashion statement. Everyone who can is copying him. Innovation is exactly that. Innovation is creating from a space where nothing existed before. You will do things differently from your competitors. You will do things differently from your friends. Different is exactly what is needed to accomplish anything new. Different is what brings about innovation.

MBE, be different. Be unique. Trailblaze. Create a reality that has never existed before. Decide your outcome. Align your actions. Meet your end goal. *Win*!

NEXT STEPS

DEFINE WHAT WINNING LOOKS LIKE for you.

1. What does winning look like for you in your business?

2. What does winning look like for you personally?

3. What is stopping you from achieving wins in your business?

4. What is stopping you from achieving wins in your personal life?

5. What steps will you implement to correct what is stopping you, or what is missing in your business that must be achieved to win?

6. What steps will you implement to correct what is stopping you, or what is missing from your personal life that must be achieved to win?

CHAPTER SIX

You Decide Your Worth: Revenue and Pricing

DR. AVIS JONES-DEWEEVER ALWAYS CONSIDERED herself a daddy's girl. In her mind, her dad, Angelo Jones, was Superman. As an entrepreneur, Dr. Jones-DeWeever could never comprehend how her father had managed to accomplish so much with such limited resources. You see, Angelo was the eldest of eight children born into a North Carolina family of sharecroppers during the period of Jim Crow laws. This was a very difficult and dangerous moment in the history of our nation, specifically for African Americans. Angelo was fourteen years old when he unexpectedly lost his own father, which required him to assume the responsibility of the man of the household. He had to make mature decisions to provide for his siblings and his mother. These decisions would not only change his life; they would also alter the legacy of Dr. Jones-DeWeever, decades before she was born.

Angelo understood the exploitative nature of the Jim Crow system and he did not want to bow to it. With only a second-grade education, he vowed never to work for anyone else again and launched his first business, a lumber company. At the time,

Black people wanted to buy homes, but nobody wanted to sell them the wood for building. Angelo's business allowed them to buy the materials they needed to build their own homes. In America, home ownership is a major foundation for wealth, so his business provided a foundation for wealth for Black families all over North Carolina.

By the time his daughter Avis was born, Angelo had grown his lumber company into a very successful business. It was so successful that he employed all of his brothers as well as a couple dozen other folks from the community. The business not only provided a comfortable life for his own family, it provided the means for his employees' families to live comfortably too.

Every week, Angelo faithfully wrote a check and gave it to his mother. In fact, he took care of her for the rest of his life. And his business success made it possible for him to finance his daughter's entire college education all the way through the completion of her PhD, paying her tuition in full so that she would never need to acquire a student loan.

Growing up, Dr. Jones-DeWeever came to understand the power, potential, and freedom that could only be afforded through entrepreneurship. Her father's legacy inspired her to one day pivot her own career and start her own business. One of the gifts her father gave her was the confidence never to feel obligated to justify her desire to start a business of her own to those closest to her, no matter how uncertain the outcome might be. She came from a family that understood: Nothing ventured is nothing gained.

She believes that if you put in the work, you can move past perceived risks. You can build entrepreneurial success that exists at a much higher level than any success you might find spending your life building somebody else's balance sheet.

For Dr. Jones-DeWeever, it was just a matter of discovering the right avenue to get there. Today, she is a media monetization mentor. She helps entrepreneurs, thought leaders, authors, and speakers leverage the power of the media to drive more leads to their business and more dollars to their bottom line. She also provides entrepreneurial training for women all over the globe.

Angelo and his daughter, Dr. Jones-DeWeever, understood their value. They understood the gap present in the market, recognized their skills and intrinsic gifts, and met the need in that market. Not only did they create opportunities for others: They pivoted their own family legacies. In this chapter we will explore how you can do the same through profitable pricing, determining your best offering, and revenue generation.

FIND A GAP AND SOLVE A PROBLEM

WHEN SHE STARTED HER BUSINESS, Dr. Jones-DeWeever realized that entrepreneurship starts with an idea that is based on the monetization of a solution. You must figure out where there is a problem and discover how that problem intersects with your zone of genius.

"At the point where the problem can be solved by your own gifts, you are able to serve as the answer to somebody's prayer," Dr. Jones-DeWeever told me when I interviewed her for this book. "You can provide a solution for someone that they've potentially been seeking for years. That, to me, is the most valuable thing you can have when you're thinking about starting a business—the one thing that you can pinpoint that's the solution."

For Dr. Jones-DeWeever, that solution came from her years of work in the realm of television, radio, publishing, and podcasting. She knew the industry and understood that many in media were narrowly focused. Many of her colleagues focused on public relations (PR). Although PR can get you television placement, this wasn't enough to change the game for most entrepreneurs. Simply showing up in media isn't enough. Businesses need the *right* kind of media attention.

"If you, as an entrepreneur, are in front of the wrong audience, you are wasting your time," Dr. Jone-DeWeever explained. "You want to make sure you are in front of the people who are looking for you, praying for you, who have a problem that *you* are the person to solve. These people are looking someplace for information to help them. What if they found you in that space where they're already looking?"

Helping people become strategic about their media acquisitions is Dr. Jones-DeWeever's zone of genius. She not only helps people with media and marketing; she also teaches them sales techniques so they can monetize opportunities. These include techniques for determining appropriate pricing and building a business with a strong revenue-generating foundation.

To create a thriving business, Dr. Jones-DeWeever identified a gap in the PR industry. She realized that the ultimate goals of her potential customers were not being met by random media placement. Her customers were not looking to be famous, but rather to grow their business. Today, she solves this problem for her clients by helping them connect to their ideal audience so they can continue to build their business and influence.

MBE, one of the best ways to ensure your success is to provide a product or service that fills a gap in the market and solves a problem. Your ability to attract customers increases exponentially if you exist in an industry that is required to purchase your products or services.

I can't tell you how many phone calls I get from excited entrepreneurs who want to tell me all about their new jewelry business. The problem is, I can already see the writing on the wall. I battle trying not to sound rude, but I really want to ask, "Do you know how many jewelry businesses are out there? Do you know how many five-dollar bracelets you will need to sell in order to make a living? Do you know how much it will cost you to advertise that product?"

Today, I hold back no more! Make sure there is a demand for your product or service. Make sure your product or service fills a gap or, as Dr. Jones-DeWeever says, answers a prayer.

Let's take the time for a little exercise. Jot down the problem your business currently solves. Then write down the answers to these questions:

- Who experiences this problem?
- How do you currently get in front of this customer?
- How do you show them that your offering is an "answered prayer"?
- If you are not currently in front of your ideal customer, what must occur for you to do so?

No answer is a bad answer. Brainstorm as many solutions as you can. Offering a product or service that is in high demand is the quickest path to building a wildly successful, cash-positive minority business enterprise!

CREATE YOUR OWN PLAYING FIELD

In my black business suit, I fit right in. I sat in the corner, far away from prying eyes, and quietly jotted down all of their secrets.

No one suspected I was a spy.

The old-timer, Baby Boomer Caucasian CPAs went on and on about paperless documentation, and casually mentioned their pricing structures, service offerings, and other inside information. Like a covert operative, I took notes on every clue to beating them at their own game.

In 2008, when everyone charged $200 per hour, I planned to undercut my competition, slash my prices in half, and charge $100 per hour. I was sure that undercutting prices was not just the easiest way, but the *only way* to compete and attract customers. And I did attract more customers—except most of them were jokers: People who paid absolutely nothing into the tax system and still got flustered and upset, even hysterical about the fact that they were not getting thousands of dollars back in refunds. Walk-in clients with illegal requests, like the ones who were actually married but filed as single even after they raved about their loving spouses and children. (They had bullied tax preparers in the past and were fully aware that they could get a larger refund, or pay less in taxes, by claiming the dishonest tax filing status of head of household and illegally hiding the fact that they were actually married.) Then there were the ones who asked me to put all the itemizations on one spouse's tax return, allowing the other spouse to claim the standard deduction, and just pretend that I did not know better. By the way, that is also illegal, folks!

All kinds of scary walked through my doors when I tried to compete on the basis of price. Although the stories are hilarious in retrospect, having to sit through someone's rant or manipulative coercion at the time just made me wish I had superpowers and could teleport the heck out of there. It only took a year for me to realize that I did not want to be a tax sweatshop. I did not want to compete with the H&R Blocks of America. I did not want to stand outside my office in the street wearing a Statue of Liberty costume in order to attract customers.

Hats off to those who do want to do this type of work; the job is definitely needed. It is not *my* jam, however. I did not enjoy working with these people. I did not feel like listening to them try to convince me to create fake companies, with fraudulent losses to offset earned income, in order to enlarge their refunds. I did not want to ignore basic Internal Revenue Service (IRS) rules for debt-financed companies. Frankly, I did not want to lose the license that I studied endless nights to obtain. These clients were not my ideal clients. I wanted clients who valued my high-net-worth tax planning specialty, customers who appreciated my thoughtful leadership and wanted to build long-term relationships.

Do you ever get a sense that you are serving the wrong market? Do you ever get a sense that your talents are just not being appreciated?

Not all customers are good customers! Not all opportunities are great opportunities! If you take the wrong customer—a bad break—not only will time spent with them suck the life out of you, it will leave you too empty and exhausted to serve the amazing customers who could provide you with an incredible future. Say no to the wrong customer. Say no to the wrong opportunity because saying no frees you up for the right opportunity.

Now you may be thinking, *But I'm a start-up. No one knows about me. They can't tell the difference between me and the shop down the street.* To you, I issue a challenge: *Make them* know about you! Make them know *all* about you. Share your amazing talents, gifts, and energy with them! And then tell them *why* they can't live without you!

Get on everyone's podcast. Give unique and innovative tips. Get videos of your customers' testimonials. Ask for referrals! Let the whole world know about you, and let them know you are not the cheapest provider out there. Make it clear that the value you provide is *phenomenal*! If this value speaks to them, if this message resonates with them, let them know that you are available to start a conversation and will get them moving in the right direction. Whatever you do, never, ever compete on price.

Never compete on price because *someone will always beat you. Someone will always be able to do it for free!* MBE, you are not in business to spend your life turning your wheels only to get nothing back! When you drop your prices to compete with your competitors, you are just joining the do-it-for-*free* brigade!

Free is just not in my vocabulary. I highly recommend you delete it from yours, too.

One of the biggest lessons I have learned is that *you* decide your worth. MBE, differentiate yourself. Stand out. Show them who you are and why they just can't live without you.

COMMAND YOUR PRICE AND KNOW YOUR MARGINS

I CAN'T TELL YOU HOW many times entrepreneurs tell me, when I first meet with them and ask how they determine their prices, that they simply copied their competitors' prices.

When you allow your competitors to dictate your prices, you allow yourself to compete in the race to give it all away for free. Price your products and services based on the *value* that you provide.

How much does it cost to bring your products and services to market? What is your break-even point? What amount of sales do you need to cover your cost of goods sold and the cost associated with bringing your product or service to market? I am not just referring to your inventory cost; I am also referring to your overhead. Overhead is the cost you incur, beyond your direct cost, that is specifically required to bring your product or service to market. Direct cost includes expenses such as materials purchased to manufacture your product, inventory you purchase to sell in your retail establishment, direct labor needed to build within a manufacturing company, and the shipping cost required to send out your customers' orders. Overhead costs include expenses outside of your direct cost, such as your general and administrative cost, the rent for your facilities, your secretary's salary, the cost of your advertising (usually a percentage of sales), the cost in utilities to keep the phone and lights on, and *your* salary. What expenses must you incur to bring your goods or services to market in the way that only you can? What is your break-even point? At what point does your revenue equal *all* of your costs? How many widgets must you sell, in other words? How many clients must you serve? How much profit do you want to make?

When I ask which expenses you must incur to bring your product or service to market, I mean the *exact* expenses. Providing a boutique-level service will cost you much more than providing an assembly-line, one-solution-fits-all service because offering a boutique-level service will require you to custom-design your solution for your end user. You will most likely spend exorbitant amounts of up-front time understanding your clients' pain points, and you may need to bring in a higher-caliber, out-of-the-box expert to perform the service. An employee required to perform a boutique-level service must be flexible, able to adjust and multitask, in order to bring the customized solution to market.

To help you determine your target revenue using the TAPs mentioned earlier, we use a Goal Seek formula in Excel to algebraically determine the desired revenue:[7]

---

[7] For additional guidance, go to https://www.SusanneMarigaCPA.com and enter your information to receive my video on how to calculate this.

Profit + Owner's Comp + Tax + Mats and Subs
+ Operating Expense = Target Revenue

Once you have calculated your target revenue, calculate the number of units that must be sold in order to achieve your Profit and Owner's Comp TAPs. You may use the formula below.

Target Revenue / Product Price = # of Units
Required to Be Sold

I also like to compute the break-even point. The break-even formula is as follows:

Break-even Point: (# of Product Sold x Cost per Product) +
Fixed Cost + Required Variable Cost = Break-even Revenue

Your fixed costs are costs that do not fluctuate from month to month. In many cases, these are either costs that must be incurred due to a contractual obligation or just a required part of your manufacturing or servicing process. An example of a fixed cost would be rent. Variable costs are costs that vary from month to month and usually vary based upon your level of production. An example of a variable cost would be the cost of electricity or other utilities.

Can you realistically sell the required numbers to produce the revenue you need in order to achieve your target allocation percentages? Or is this a long trail to disappointment? Sometimes a product or service is so commoditized that it is very difficult to achieve a desired profit, simply because the volume it takes to achieve the desired revenue is greater than market demand.

Remember Chris, the staffing agency client I mentioned in Chapter 4? Chris has a heart of gold. He is a man who takes pride in his work and only wants to super-serve his customers. He is proud to provide opportunities within his community.

Pre-Profit First, no matter how many millions of dollars in revenue he generated, Chris was unable to get his head above water. Cash was constantly tight. Profits were constantly negative. No matter how hard he sold or how many sales he made, the results were the same: *negative*. He had fallen into the trap of trading margins for volume.

Chris believed that if he just sold more at a low price point, he would produce profits. What he hadn't considered is that increasing sales volume correlates with an increase in cost. As his sales increased, his general administrative costs did too. Then, because of increased sales, he required more recruiters, a larger office space, more computers, and more software licenses. What was initially a negative profit just continued to compound. This compounding of negative margins continued until Chris ran a million-dollar loss. Eventually no bank would lend to him, and the cash just ran out.

That is what happens when you trade margins for volume. As you increase revenue and sales, the cost in terms of general and administrative (G&A) expenses increases in proportion. Many people mistakenly think of G&A as fixed costs. They don't consider that, as a business grows and scales, rent, utilities, and administrative labor costs also grow in proportion to the revenue. When your business is small, you may only need one administrative person and a small warehouse building. As it grows, you may likely require more support staff, more salespeople, and maybe even a commercial warehouse.

Always remember: The cost to run your business will increase with your sales volume. When budgeting for an increase in revenue, calculate G&A as a percentage of this revenue. This way, when you budget for an increase in revenue, you can expect there to be an increase in G&A.

Excel has an amazing tool called Goal Seek, which is very helpful in calculating expenses with proportional changes in revenue for various scenarios. This analysis will help you derive the actual cost and revenue associated with achieving your profit goals.

IMPROVE YOUR MARGINS

SOME BUSINESSES JUST PRODUCE HIGHER margins—period. In a manufacturing company, it may be easy to accumulate a million dollars in sales simply because you are able to sell more items wholesale, but the gross margins of this business, in most cases, are tiny. In manufacturing, not only do you have a higher up-front cost to build out the initial infrastructure, you must also sell a higher volume of product just to break even. In effect, a lot more work, energy, and strategy go into building a profitable manufacturing company.

However, a service-based business, depending on the service, may produce higher margins from the start. Once you have taken care of your initial education requirements, you can sell your accumulated knowledge, your ideas, and your creative implementation of those ideas. Brain-capital ventures require lower up-front cost and initial capital investment than traditional manufacturing companies. And the margins in a service-based industry are much higher. It is not uncommon for a service-based industry to charge three to four times its direct labor cost.

In Profit First, we recommend that each full-time employee generate a minimum of $150,000 in Real Revenue. For industries involving higher-earning professionals such as physicians, attorneys, or engineers, we expect this ratio of Real Revenue to employee to be much higher. It is recommended that each direct labor employee generate a minimum of three times their cost. I prefer at least four times the cost, as this ratio allows for meeting target allocation percentages with ease. You need a ratio like this in place in order to pay the employee, cover non-billable time, recoup overhead, and, most importantly, incur a profit.

When starting a business, owners should first consider what their gifts are. What can they do better—and bring to market better—than anyone else? What are their innate talents?

If you are an engineer, can you solve a problem in a better way than most in your field? If you are a doctor, can you heal a certain ailment better than most others can? What is it that you do better than anyone else? Businesses that spring from these gifts are usually the easiest businesses to start with the greatest profit margins. Honor your innate gifts. Consider a niche specialization. You will find profits within your destiny.

Now, manufacturing is crucial to our economy. Without our manufacturers, we would not enjoy the quality of life that we have today in America. Our coffee mugs, our paper plates, our watches—anything that we can physically touch is a gift from our production companies. There is a place in our society for these businesses.

It will take most manufacturing companies a lot more in terms of sales to achieve the same profits as their serviced-based industry counterparts. So an important question for those of you who are gifted in the production of physical goods and materials is, how can you bring your goods to market at the best quality *and* the lowest cost?

Is forming partnerships overseas an option for you? Can you find a manufacturing partner who can produce your goods and services more efficiently and more effectively, but at the same quality that you can and while reducing your overall cost? Have you considered a co-packer? A co-packer is a third-party manufacturer that both produces and packages goods for their clients. Forming partnerships with those who can do this better than you will enable you to bring your creativity into physical form at a reduced cost. Then you will be able to scale and achieve a lower break-even cost. Thus, profit will be easier to achieve.

This is about operating more efficiently: working smarter, not harder. Form quality partnerships, reduce risk, and reduce cost! Excellent work, MBE!

THE SPARK WITHIN YOU

I WANT THIS BOOK TO be for the people and about the people: a book that not only serves our communities, but also champions the stories of our heroes. While writing this book, I had the opportunity to interview some pretty amazing entrepreneurs. One of the questions I asked each of these entrepreneurs is: If you could offer one piece of advice to the next up-and-coming, rising MBE, what would it be?

When I asked this question of Dr. Avis, she said: "Trust that spark. What I'm referring to is, I truly believe that each and every individual is born with a spark within them that is unique to only them. That means that you're the only person in the world who has your spark. When you leave this world, that spark will go with you. I think that your business is a reflection of that spark. It's a reflection of your purpose.

"Oftentimes, as entrepreneurs, we're a different crew. We're different people. The thing is, nobody else is going to see that spark but you. Nobody else feels it but you. Nobody else can see the vision that you have in your head but you. It's oftentimes the case that we're around a lot of individuals who we care about, and who care about us, but they think that they're doing us a favor when they try to hold us back, to keep us on a safe path, to have us not chase that thing that they can't see. Here's the thing: they're not supposed to see it. It's for *you* to see. It's my belief that it is if it's in your head, if it's in your heart, if it was given to you, that spark is your gift and it's your responsibility to grow it and to nourish it such that it develops into this huge flame that everybody in the world can see because of your good work. It is your responsibility to do it.

"To me, that means that even in those moments when the people who love you are trying to diminish your spark, trying to snuff it out, smother it, you know that it is yours. You have to protect it. You can love them, but don't love them to the point where they diminish your purpose, because that is your gift to the world. That is your destiny to fulfill. So, believe in it. When you believe in it, focus on it, invest in it, grow it. Then, I guarantee you, you will meet with success."

MAKE YOUR OWN TABLE

WHEN I WAS GROWING UP, my family sat at the dinner table each night to share a meal. Some nights, my dad came home after an especially hard day seeming discouraged and ate his dinner in silence.

Then, out of nowhere, he would look at us kids disapprovingly and say the words I shared with you in Chapter 1: "You are Black kids, and as Black people you will need to work twice as hard and be twice as good as any of these white people just to be able to sit at the table."

His was a hard rant to hear. In fact, in many ways it probably left scars on all of his offspring. When there is no light at the end of tunnel, no best that we can't beat, we are left to outdo where we were the day before. And at the end of the day, nothing we do is good enough. Better is always a moving target we can't reach. That is why, MBE, it is so important to define what winning looks like for you.

Most of my childhood occurred in the '80s and early '90s. On March 3, 1991, Rodney King, a Black man, was brutally beaten by Los Angeles Police Department (LAPD) officers after a high-speed chase, during an arrest for drunk driving. Televisions around the country showed continual footage of an unarmed King lying on the ground as LAPD officers used excessive force to beat him. At this time in American history, positive role models of African American doctors (with one exception, the fictional character played by Bill Cosby) were not depicted in the media. We were only three generations removed from slavery. My dad was simply speaking his truth. He was passing the wisdom he had learned, based on the experiences he had witnessed and the disrespect that had been inflicted upon him, down to us children. Dad was simply paying the knowledge forward.

Sad to say, today—forty years later—many of the features of his reality are still present. As our nation pivots through the Black Lives Matter movement, the inequities still exist. I hope that, by leveling the playing field and creating opportunities, we MBEs have the opportunity to change this legacy for generations to come. By competing based on *quality*, not price, we will command our due respect regardless of our race, creed, religion, gender, or sexual orientation.

MBE, when we work twice as hard as the status quo demands and earn our place in the world as thought leaders, we don't merely earn a place at the table. We create our own table.

In entrepreneurship, you have the freedom to be everything you want to be. The market has the potential to promote, support, and bring you forward. There has never been a better time for minority business enterprises to bring their products or services to market in America.

Even in the midst of stereotypes, you can shine and show the world just how intelligent and creative you are! With advancements in technology, including online video platforms such as YouTube, social media, and online conference tools, you've never had better access to a wider audience. You can show America how great you are with ease.

I wrote this book during the initial shelter-in-place period of COVID-19. Everyone—and I mean everyone, except for essential retail, healthcare, and government employees—was in lockdown. After the ten o'clock news ended, I lay in bed watching *Jimmy Kimmel Live!* Not only was Jimmy Kimmel still broadcasting at night: he had also started filming daily from his home. He often filmed his adorable kids for the show. (I've seen his home so much, now, I know what his couch looks like.)

During the same week, my accounting firm, Mariga CPA, launched our live show on Facebook. We livestreamed to hundreds of viewers, teaching them our playbook as part of our "Profit First Master Class with Susanne Mariga" group.

When I replay the show now (maybe I am being a little full of myself), I see that we are just as funny, just as entertaining as Jimmy Kimmel. Our viewers return day after day to watch the newest show. In fact, they are such die-hards that they actually comment in the chat during rebroadcasts!

With today's technology, you can compete with *Jimmy Kimmel Live!* You can get your message out there. You can broadcast what makes you different. You can own the space!

In fact, I would even dare to say that it is easier for an MBE to own the space now, thanks to virtual technology. The barriers of entry we once faced, ranging from slavery to discrimination to ridicule of accents or vernacular, are either gone or changing, and the old mindsets are shifting toward equality. The cost of technology needed to get our message out into the world (a webcam, a mic, and a computer) is now incredibly low. If we can say something captivating, say something different, and keep our audience entertained, we have the opportunity to not only capture the space, but also capture the attention of the masses!

You can shine just as brightly as Jimmy Kimmel! You no longer need network approval to air your show. You can do it directly on YouTube. You can do it directly in your Facebook group. Heck, you can even create an industry group in Facebook! Embrace technology. MBE, dare to be different. Innovate, create, and bring yourself to the market in a way that's never been seen before.

NEXT STEPS

IN SUMMARY, MBE, YOU WANT to operate a business that is in demand. You want to price your product in accordance not only with the cost incurred to bring the product to market, but also based upon the quality that you are able to provide.

For this exercise, please perform the following steps:

1. Identify the problem that your product or service solves.

2. Identify the ideal customer to target for this product.

3. Identify the fixed costs associated with bringing this product or service to market.

4. Identify the variable costs. This can be the cost per widget or cost of goods sold per item sold.

5. Calculate your break-even point: # of Product Sold x Cost per Product + Fixed Cost + Required Variable Cost = Break-even Revenue

6. Calculate your target revenue: Profit + Owner's Comp + Tax + Mats and Subs + Required Operating Expense = Target Revenue

CHAPTER SEVEN

The Illusion of Millions: Government Contracts

IN THE FALL OF 2008, I attended a random governmental request for proposal (RFP) conference knowing full well that my company would have zero chance of ever winning this contract—we were too small and too new ever to be seriously considered. Although I had the right background in governmental accounting from my work at KPMG, and experience in composing Comprehensive Annual Financial Reports (CAFRs), I knew this contract was way, way bigger than me. However, I had nothing to lose and everything to gain. I figured, heck, why not? Why not attend the RFP meeting? I could see what these meetings are all about, and when the time came for me to bid, I would at least know how to present myself. So I hired a babysitter for my chubby little girl, packed my briefcase, put on a business suit, and went.

When I arrived at the RFP meeting, I found the purchasing committee sitting in a stodgy-looking board room. Formally suited, perched on a judge's bench, each of them appeared stiff. To the eyes of a newcomer, they seemed a bit intimidating. The purchasing committee exchanged greetings with those they already knew. Feeling shy, I sat quietly and observed the new environment. Interestingly, the board room was pretty empty. In fact, besides me, only one was present. It was definitely not the room, chock-full of bidders, where I had expected to hide.

Whether it was how I dressed, how I presented myself, or how I answered the questions, I must have made a good impression that day. Although I was not awarded the contract, the prime contractor eventually asked me to assist them with another contract.

Although they may hire subcontractors to assist in the completion of a project, the prime contractor is selected by the governmental entity to ensure that the project is completed in its entirety. To help reach diversity initiative spending goals, many large government contracts require that the prime contractor select a minority- or woman-owned business enterprise as a subcontractor for a portion of the project.

Sometimes, opportunities show up when you communicate to the universe that you are ready to receive them. One of the biggest lessons I have learned is that, as John C. Maxwell says, "Sometimes you win, and sometimes you learn." MBE, there is a gift in every experience. Even if the job is way too big for you, even if there is no chance in the world that it will be awarded to you, when the universe presents an opportunity from which you will benefit, take it. You never know where it will lead you.

Being present for this opportunity that was way bigger than me at the time gave me the right exposure and experience to later build a government practice of my own. This also led to some key learnings in regard to discerning the difference between a good opportunity and a great opportunity. Honing this skill of discernment saved me both future dollars and time.

THE CONSEQUENCES OF WINNING

CHRIS, WHOM YOU MET IN Chapter 4, had government contracts. Lots of them. Each RFP included a request that he list his price, and clearly stated that the governmental purchasing committees responsible for selection would choose the proposal with the best value. Best value is the best combination of price, experience, and offering. Chris, eager to present his proposals as those with best value, offered the government the moon and stars—in exchange for which, he also offered the purchasing committee a price only slightly above his cost.

Chris's goal was to win the contracts at all costs. His strategy was to offer a price below that of each and every competitor; after all, these were multimillion-dollar contracts. Surely, he believed, he would earn a profit on the volume. Even if he just earned a small percentage, this profit would at least be a million, right? The problem Chris faced was that negative margins plus negative margins only beget more negative margins. Remember: When you deal with multimillion-dollar contracts, you also deal with the probability of million-dollar losses.

Michelle, whom you met in Chapter 1, had the most lucrative contracts around. Her company serviced U.S. military bases around the world, and her janitorial services were considered the best. Her contracts were in the millions. When she priced her contracts, she did so based on the square footage of the surface area her company would be required to clean. Michelle's price was also based upon the price offered by the last contractor. This previous price was a coveted number that Michelle had obtained from the prior contractor's bid tabulation. Based on the historical winning bid, Michelle designed a markup slightly higher than the cost for her to complete the job. She did so because she understood that this was a volume-based business. After all, in a million-dollar contract, there had to be some left over for her.

Michelle hammered the need for efficiency into her staff. She obsessively tracked her janitors' hours, searched high and low for the lowest-cost administrative personnel, and found every possible cost to cut.

As a result of her militant management style, Michelle experienced excessive turnover in her staff. The pressure to clean fast, and for managers to keep everyone in line, was overwhelming. Michelle was never a fun person to be around. Although she is naturally a very nice gal and means only the best, the people she worked with never saw those qualities. They often complained that they felt stressed when they were around her. Many trusted, quality employees quit at the earliest opportunity.

For all the millions of dollars in contracts that Michelle received, she never took home a salary of more than $100,000. Her profitability was usually negative. The salary she did receive was reinvested into the business. From preparing Michelle's tax return year after year, I found that her husband, a mechanic, was really the hero of the family. He supported the family financially.

MBE, be aware that though government contracts may be for millions of dollars, they do not equate to millions of dollars in *profit*.

PROCUREMENT: KNOW THE DEVIL YOU'RE DEALING WITH

ONE BLACK FRIDAY, I WENT shopping with a dear friend of mine, a procurement manager for a large oil and gas company. She is one of the best in her field. We went to the outlet malls. I love these malls because they have all the designer brands that make my friends squeal in delight but at oh-so-satisfying discounts that allow me to buy wonderful gifts at prices way below market. Black Friday outlet mall shopping has become one of my family's favorite traditions.

On this particular Black Friday, my friend and I both swore to spend the same amount of money. We acknowledged the necessity of limitations and promised to be accountability partners. We were going to be good, disciplined shoppers, stay on task, and get all of our holiday shopping done in one night.

As we entered the crowded stores filled with shoppers, I was overcome by excitement about the sales. We went to the OskKosh B'gosh. The Coach Store. The Kate Spade Store. Even Neiman Marcus. With every purchase I made, I believed I was getting a good deal. I was finding once-in-a-lifetime steals.

At the end of the night (really, the next morning), my friend and I collapsed on a bench in utter exhaustion. As we sat in the middle of the commotion of the outlet complex and compared our loot, a dark realization came upon me. My friend—my dear friend—was not only a highly skilled procurement manager: She was also an undercover shopping assassin. She had purchased twice as many things as I had, but paid only half the amount I had laid out. Even worse, her purchases were actually *cuter* and of higher quality.

I had forgotten that procurement specialists are trained to do exactly that: *procure.* They are trained both to procure at the lowest possible price and to obtain the highest possible value. They will complete this mission at *your* expense.

MBE, if you cannot make a profit in line with your TAPs on a project, it is not worth your time to complete the RFP. If you know that the current contractor is offering the government a price that you will not be able to beat or will not be able to beat with a *profit*, it is better for you to let the opportunity go. Wait for the incumbent to go out of business, or claim bankruptcy; only then will you be able to bid at a fair price.

Now, some of you MBEs are probably thinking, *But government contracts, we've been told, are the way to go.* This can be true. Governments even have certification programs that incentivize procurement requests for minority business enterprises. My response to you is to remember my friend, the procurement manager, and remember that, as sweet as she is, she is a trained financial assassin. Once you are in a contract, you are in a *contract*. Contracts are difficult to break. More than one minority business enterprise has ended up financing a government's (and prime contractor's) endeavor. By the time they realize they are on a sinking ship, their line of credit is exhausted, *they* are exhausted, and some are on the brink of bankruptcy.

WHEN IS A GOVERNMENT CONTRACT A GOOD OPPORTUNITY?

THIS QUESTION IS USUALLY THE next question I get, so I will answer it. A government contract is good when you are allowed to do your best work at a price that will give you a profit in line with your TAPs. These are not usually low-end contracts, but rather highly specialized, and vendors are selected based unique skill sets.

The best contracts are sole source contracts. A little-known fact is that many sole source contracts do not even go out for bid. The RFP process is not used for these contracts because it is assumed that the service or product is so specialized that only one provider can meet the obligation.

Some examples of goods and services obtained by sole source contracts are specialized component parts made by a specific manufacturing company; select research projects; and specialized niche accounting, engineering, or technical projects. I think you are seeing the trend here. *Specialized.* Meaning that not everyone can do the work. The people who can went to school for their specialties and are known throughout their industries as specialists in their areas. For the most part, they are fully entrenched professionals; this is all they do. Many of these contractors also have pre-existing relationships with both the procurement managers and the departmental contract managers in their industries. They have rubbed shoulders with these managers at industry-specific conferences and are members of the same trade associations. They have most likely presented on their specialties.

By the time an RFP is issued and the silent period has commenced—if indeed there is an RFP for a given sole source project, as, again, many do not even require a bid—the specialist vendor knows that they are more than likely to win the contract.

MBE, do not waste your time responding to an RFP that you do not have a good chance of winning. Do not allow the government to steal the ideas presented in your proposal and use them with another vendor. Do not waste your time responding to an RFP that will not allow you to price your goods or services in accordance with your target allocation percentages! MBE, if you compete solely on price, someone will always beat you out for the contract. I have learned to love using the words "no bid" as part of my email response to an RFP.[8]

In summary, not all opportunities are good opportunities. Beware of trading margins for volume. When a contract appears lucrative due to the potential for large revenue, make sure that the profits are in line with your target allocation percentages. Otherwise, you may find that taking this contract will tie up your resources, preventing you from taking on more profitable ventures.

---

[8] I have an amazing video about what happens when you trade margins for volume on my Profit First with Susanne Mariga YouTube Channel. By the way, go ahead and subscribe to the channel. I regularly release new content regarding Profit First. https://www.youtu.be/TqDrE0g38aM

NEXT STEPS

WHEN EVALUATING THE POTENTIAL OF an RFP, consider the following:

1. Can you achieve your TAPs based upon your bid amount?

2. Total Revenue – Mats and Subs = Tax + Profit + Owner's Comp + OPEX

3. Can you achieve this target revenue and operate comfortably without being forced to use the cheapest labor, or highly discounted equipment?

4. Can you bring your product or service to market for this contract, for the price you are offering, in a way that makes you feel proud?

If you answer no to any of these questions, invoke the Monopoly rule: Do not pass go. Better opportunities await you. Your competitor—the one who took the government contract— will not have the resources to compete with you. They will be too busy serving the low-end contract.

CHAPTER EIGHT

Expenses = Stewardship

WHEN I THINK OF EXPENSES, I focus on stewardship and return on investment (ROI). Stewardship is about considering: What will I do with the resources God has given me? How will I use these resources to multiply them and serve His cause?

No matter our faith, our businesses are the gifts with which we are entrusted. They are the vehicles that allow us to do good in the world and impact others in a way that most never have the opportunity to do, under normal circumstances.

Our businesses allow us to provide employment and opportunities for those who might never get such breaks otherwise. When we do this, we become a gift and ally to our communities and our nations.

MBE, I love the Bible. It has so many great stories—and lessons about managing people. The story of Moses, and how he had to manage all of those Israelites for forty years in the wilderness, still confounds me. Personally, I think I would have fired everyone and walked off the job if I were Moses. Good thing God picked the right man for the job.

When I think of stewardship, I think of one of the Biblical stories from Matthew 25:14-30, NIV. In this story, there is a man of great wealth who, like many men of great wealth, realizes that he cannot continue to grow his kingdom without the assistance of a team.

In order to continue to grow his territory, this man realized that he needed to leave his kingdom and explore new ventures. The man had three servants. He also had eight bags of gold. He entrusted his gold to his servants while he was away.

To the first servant, he gave five bags of gold. To the next, he gave two bags of gold. And to the last servant, he gave one bag of gold.

Scripture says that the man allocated the resources to each servant *based upon their abilities*. He didn't just give each of them a random number of bags. He looked at each servant and thought, *What can you handle? What can I safely entrust you with? What has your history been with me?* He then allocated his resources based upon each servant's individual ability.

I am sure this wealthy man was anxious when he returned from his trip. Any one of us would be nervous if we had to entrust all our resources to our team. I am sure it felt like leaving a car with your teenager for the very first time. Just plain scary.

Upon the man's return, he met his first servant.

The first servant was thrilled to see his master. He proudly and quickly informed the wealthy man that although he been left with just five bags of gold, he had made some seriously smart moves. This servant was clever. He was quick on his feet. Instead of allowing the money to sit idle, he had invested it and now reaped the rewards of doubling his master's investment! The wealthy man now had ten bags of gold.

Pleased and excited, the master patted his servant on the back and said, "Well done, good and faithful servant. You have been faithful with a few things; I will put you in charge of many things. Come and share your master's happiness."

The master then met with the second servant, who had received two bags of gold. He too was eager to see his master return.

When this servant saw his master approach, he ran to greet him and said, "Look master, you have entrusted me with two bags of gold, see, I have gained two more."

Again, pleased, the master looked at him and said, "Well done, good and faithful servant! You have been faithful with a few things; I will put you in charge of many. Come and share your master's happiness."

The wealthy man remembered that he still had one bag of gold left. The third servant, however, was nowhere in sight. After some inquiries, the master was able to locate him. As the master approached the third servant, the servant began to quiver. The master then inquired about the status of his gold.

The servant replied, "Master, I know you are a hard man… harvesting where you have not sown and gathering where you have not scattered seed." Talk about rambling! These kinds of people always have excuses. The more they talk, the more they frustrate the tar out of me!

The servant continued, "So I was afraid and went out and hid your gold in the ground. But here is what belongs to you…" The servant held out the single bag of gold to his master. The older man stood in silent disbelief.

Then the master shouted, "You wicked, lazy servant! You knew that I harvest where I have not sown and gather where I have not scattered seed? Well then, you should have deposited with the banks, so that when I returned, I would have at least received some interest."

In anger, the master grabbed the bag of gold from the servant. He gave the gold to the servant with the ten bags.

The Bible then reads, "Whoever has will be given more, and they will have abundance. Whoever does not have, even what they have will be taken from them."

The master threw the worthless servant outside into the darkness.

Which servant are you? Are you the one entrusted with five bags of gold who will grow your resources into ten bags of gold? Or are you the third, who will simply bury your talents and live out of fear and scarcity? What type of harvest will you reap? MBE, to run a wildly successful, profitable business, you must practice *stewardship*!

Stewardship is not just about money. Stewardship also includes how you use your talents and your time. As human beings, we are all given the same amount of time in a day. We are all given three hundred and sixty-five days a year, twenty-four hours a day and seven days a week. No one, no matter how precious they are, will receive one second more.

Why do some people just seem to accomplish more in the same amount of time? Why do some people climb more mountains, build bigger empires, and create greater change? The answer, my friend, is stewardship. They simply take advantage of the resources they have and look for opportunities to grow their resources.

In this chapter, we will discuss an important element of stewardship: how to evaluate your expenses in order to achieve your target allocation profit level.

REVIEW YOUR FINANCIAL STATEMENTS

WHEN EVALUATING YOUR LEVEL OF stewardship, I recommend that you start with reviewing your financial statements. I am always amazed by how many business owners do not maintain up-to-date financial statements. When they tell me that they don't even have financial statements, I often stare in confusion. I am left wondering how they make business decisions when they don't know how much money they make or how they are spending it. If you don't receive financial statements on a regular basis, I think we have a problem. Call your Profit First Professional *now*.[9] Obtain your financial statements. You must know where you are today to create the plan of action that will take you where you are going.

As you analyze your financial statements, determine: How are you wasting money? Is every dollar spent serving you? Is your hard-earned money getting you to your greater purpose?

You'd be surprised how many business owners I meet every year who tell me that they just give their bank statements to their accountant or bookkeeper, who then returns the statements to them. These entrepreneurs will then confess that they have

---

[9] If you don't have a Profit First Professional, you can find one at https://www.ProfitFirstProfessionals.com.

no understanding of the financial statements or how to use them. It is even more interesting to meet the ones who purchase an online accounting software subscription for forty dollars a month. These business owners often hire a bookkeeper or accountant to enter their financial data into the system. However, they never take that next step and actually log into the software. These entrepreneurs are not taking advantage of the opportunities afforded them!

Financial statements and systems exist so that you can make pertinent decisions in real time. If you don't understand your numbers, if you don't log in and use the reports generated by the system for anything beyond getting your taxes prepared, you are wasting money. If the system is confusing to you, invest the time with your accountant to better understand how it works. If the system is too archaic, then invest and get another one! Whatever you do, MBE, do not waste your money or lose opportunities to make critical decisions.

So many software programs now allow you to import your income statement into an Excel spreadsheet. You can then sort the columns any way you please. Sort your expenses from largest to smallest. I suggest you tackle the smallest ones first. (I am all about the easy wins—the early victories and the greatest motivators!) Look at your dues and memberships. Are you even attending the meetings regularly? Are you learning anything from these organizations that will help you grow your business or service your clients? Do these organizations bring in business for you? Do you even believe in the purpose of these organizations? Are your memberships on auto renewal, so you fail to cancel them either because you forget or don't have time to call? (Or maybe you don't have the heart to break bad news.) Don't let inattentiveness result in a vicious circle of waste.

After you address your lowest expenses, move on the next lowest. I recommend reviewing your financial statements via your software. Double-click on the hyperlink if your software allows you to do this. View the actual expenses listed under the summarized expense amount. What expenses does the line item *really* represent?

Let's talk about rent expenses. Sometimes we are locked into what seem like near-permanent fixed costs. These fixed costs often include our leases and contractual commitments. For many, removing these expenses or decreasing them is not an overnight process. It requires a slow, gradual, strategic plan.

With regard to leases, I want you to think about your long-term strategy. With the most recent technological advancements, office space is, in many cases, becoming obsolete. Teleconferencing software as a service (SAS) application provides the impact of face-to-face meetings while significantly reducing the need for office space, airfare, hotels, and even commuting. If used well, technology can create a sense of community that even face-to-face interactions can't reach due to bias and introversion.

What is your long-term goal? Do you have the ability to go virtual? Do you want to create an environment in which you can recruit from among the best and brightest not only within your community, but around the world? How would having more square footage increase your revenue and your profits? What will you do if you outgrow the space before the lease ends? Even more importantly, what will you do if you experience significant revenue loss before the lease agreement ends? How important is it to you to be able to remain flexible? These are all questions you must consider when evaluating your current lease agreements, and especially before entering a new lease agreement.

Again, think about your long-term goals. What do you envision for yourself and your company within the next five years? Within the next ten? What will your business look like? Who will you be? Personally, I want to work from a remote island. Hey, MBE, we all need to have a dream! What is yours?

The next thing I consider when I review all of the line items on the P&L statement is the return on investment (ROI) for each expense. This means I consider what the offsetting gain will be for each expense I incur.

Each time I review my financial statements, I expect to see at least small gains in revenue, profit, and time. I ask myself: Does this expense propel my revenue, increase my profit, or just give me more time? Does this expense free me up to do more things, so that I can grow more revenue, so that I can increase my profit? How does this expense serve me?

FOR MORE PROFITS, HIRE THE BEST AND BRIGHTEST

PAYROLL IS A TRICKY ISSUE. At some point, we may come to a place where the employee we hired when we first started out no longer serves us. Perhaps before we grew, we were a much simpler organization. Now we require a more intricate specialty. Perhaps, as we specialized, we found that we require a true problem-solver. Maybe in the beginning we could tolerate an employee whose abilities were limited to copying steps one by one, but over time, as we became more specialized, we realized we must fix what is broken. Fixing what is broken always requires a specialized skill. Whatever the cause, the team we have may no longer serve us!

It is said that one "A" player equals three "B" players. Three "B" players equal six "C" players. The more "A" players you have on your team, the less players you will need. Hire more "A" players.

When I analyze my payroll expense, I typically start with a list of all my employees. I sort them by salary, with my highest earner (myself) first. I truly believe that "for unto whomsoever much is given, of him shall be much required." (Luke 12:48, KJV).

Each day, I must earn my clients' trust and business. Each day, my employees should be helping me continue to do so. I have to consider: Is this person helping me move toward my cause and my company's goals? Is this person giving it their all? Are they still interested in the work that they are doing? Do they have passion? Are they contributing to the team as a whole? If, over the years, I observe that their passion has waned and their productivity has lessened, it becomes time to ask the big question: Would it be better for me to let them go and allow them to find their own piece of happiness in this world? This is where the term mercy firing comes into play.

Is this person still a fit for my team? With respect to the waning performance question, would encouragement, training, and feedback spur them back into motion? Is this relationship salvageable, or will I just be better off parting ways with them and replacing them with someone who is better suited to do their job?

Human resources management is one of the hardest aspects of business to tackle. So much about our interactions with our team is deeply rooted in psychology and mindset. Sometimes, the best way to tackle an organizational chart is just to step away, remove all the emotion, and look at yourself as a friend who desperately needs advice. Would you tell your best friend to keep this employee, or would you tell your best friend to run for the hills as fast as they can? How would you counsel your best friend if they were in this situation? You deserve honest feedback from your *internal* best friend.

You are your most valuable player. Just as you should be your highest-paid employee, your team should support your leadership with their best! If necessary, imagine your team without this person. Would the whole team be better off? Take a weekend to veg out and process your decision, but do not let a bad thing fester.

In Matthew 5:30, KJV, the Bible says, "If thy right hand offend thee, cut if off and cast it from thee; for it is profitable for thee that one of thy members should perish, and not that thy whole body should be cast into hell."

Do not allow your organization to be stunted by your loyalty to an employee who can to can no longer serve you! Pluck them out! You already know that I love the Bible. It is a great source of wisdom. When it comes to scaling and managing a business, keep no bad employee! Allowing mediocrity to remain in your organization will make your organization mediocre.

You can only run as fast as the pace of your slowest runner. As long as you keep poor performers in your mist, your company's performance will be limited. Someone will always have to stop and clean up a mess. Someone will always need to do more to overcompensate for the someone who does less. You will continually lose your "A" players if you coddle your "C" players, because *anyone* will get tired of cleaning up these messes at some point!

Galatians 5:9, NIV, says, "A little yeast works through the whole batch of dough." This applies to both stagnation and regression. It just takes a little "bad" to ruin it for the whole. Keep only the *great* and you will build a wildly profitable and fulfilling company.

MAKE THE NECESSARY CHANGES TO AFFORD YOUR TEAM

I MET DAN AND BILL in May of 2018. They had started a janitorial company two years before, and they absolutely loved what they did. They loved leaving every home and corporate building glistening. They loved the smell of disinfectants. When the carpet was tidy and freshly vacuumed, they felt that their work in this world was *done*!

As their business grew, Dan and Bill hired employees. Like many business owners taught by their local Small Business Administrations (SBAs), they believed that to scale a business, you need to bring in new employees. There is a tantalizing pressure to create jobs in small-business America. However, Dan and Bill came to a point where they earned $300,000 in revenue annually and carried six employees on the payroll, but had not taken a paycheck themselves for over two years. They were disgusted with their company's finances, disheartened by their situation, and, as a result of all of this negativity, were quite plainly no fun to be around anymore. Even worse, everyone in the company was constantly busy, including Dan and Bill.

Dan and Bill had two problems. They had six full-time employees living off of $300,000 in revenue—eight full-time employees, if you include the owners. Although they kept costs down by working out of their homes, Dan and Bill were still required to carry insurance, purchase supplies, and reimburse their employees, who traveled to client sites to perform the services. They also incurred advertising expenses, as they believed they had to let the world know they were out there. You can do the math. Splitting what was left of $300,000 after operating costs between eight employees meant that every employee, including Dan and Bill, was living below the poverty line!

Cash was tight and Dan and Bill were stuck in a cycle. Although they desperately wanted to hire a supervisor, they could not afford it. Although they did not want to work every single waking minute of their lives, they just could not break free. They could not up-level their team because no job candidate in the market was willing to work for free—nor, quite frankly, should they. Dan and Bill had a big problem. They simply were not charging enough for the services they brought to the market. In addition, they had far too many employees on their payroll.

I recommended that Dan and Bill raise their prices and reduce head count by retaining only the most efficient of team players.

We performed a job-cost analysis, reviewed their profitability by job, and determined which jobs were being financed by the really great and profitable contracts. Then, we canceled the poorly performing contracts by offering to continue to work with clients only if they accepted an increase in price. Weak, money-draining contracts showed themselves to the door, so to speak. Dan and Bill were surprised that most clients stayed with them and accepted the price increase. Most clients know when they are getting a deal. The guilt over receiving such a great deal won't move them to ask you to allow them to pay more. Only you can represent your own best interest.

CONSIDER LOWER-COST ALTERNATIVES

WHEN YOU REVIEW YOUR EXPENSES, consider lower-cost alternatives. Can the service be completed by a lower-cost provider? Does another service to which you currently subscribe provide an overlapping service? If this is the case, would consolidating these services into one platform not only create ease of access, but reduce overall cost? You may have to take the time to do a little research, but this research will probably add noteworthy cash to your pocket.

One thing I think governmental entities have mastered is a process called competitive bidding. In this process, once an expense exceeds an established threshold, governments are required to issue a request for proposal (RFP) in order to select the vendor who offers the best value. Best value is the best combination of both price and offering. In order to protect their constituents, governments have implemented some hefty compliance rules. In many cases, administrations are required to comply with a silence period in which no proposing vendor is allowed to contact anyone on the purchasing committee. The final bid submission is not known until the date and time when the administration has announced all sealed bids will be opened. This is done to protect the integrity of the bidding process. It allows for a free, ethical, and competitive process.

I would not recommend that small business owners invest the time necessary to do the kind of extensive procurement process that the government does. However, I think it might be a worthwhile investment to seek out at least three bids for any major purchase. Not only will reviewing different vendors allow you to see what is readily available for you in the market, it will also allow you to evaluate your pricing options. I bet that by making this your policy, you will reduce the overall cost of a number of expenses.

We live in Houston, Texas. The winters are wonderful here. However, the summers are so hot you could probably fry an egg on the pavement. When we got our first energy bill in this house, our eyeballs nearly popped out of our heads. A whopping $500 in the middle of July—we couldn't believe it. We were only home in the evenings and on weekends. This bill was equal to the entire monthly cost of the apartment we had rented just a few months before.

My husband, Jeffrey, is a geologist. He immediately began to research different energy companies. A few years earlier, the local, major energy company had been forced to demonopolize. Now smaller energy companies, utilizing the former monopoly's infrastructure, resold its electricity. Jeffrey researched fixed-rate energy plans, variable-rate energy plans, even plans that offered nights and weekends free. That year, he decided to go with a fixed-rate plan. Although locking us into a contract was a gamble, he felt that we were adequately hedging our risk. He reasoned that though the bill might be higher in certain months, we would see a long-term benefit, especially during the summer months. The following July, our bill was around $250, almost half of what it had been the year before.

Each year, Jeffrey conducts his research and studiously compares various vendors, and each year he has been successful in keeping our energy bill low. Our energy bill is lower than that of most homes in the area, even after we had two kids.

MBE, seek out competitive bids on your major expenses. There are riches to be found in the research.

STABILIZE YOUR PROFIT WITH MATS AND SUBS

FOR MY MANUFACTURERS, MY RETAILERS, my construction contractors, and those in any line of business that has traditional direct cost, this part is for you!

Although you may have some room for negotiation if you are able to make large volume purchases, there is often very little wiggle room to reduce price in the mats and subs category. For the most part, market demand determines these rates. If you are unable or unwilling to purchase at market rate, the inventory (especially the hot, high-turnover items) will just be sold to someone else. The best subcontractors simply won't work for you. These subcontractors know you are not the only builder in town. They realize that they can go down the street, hang out at Home Depot, and earn more working for another general contractor (GC). After all, who has time to haggle with someone who won't recognize the value they bring to the table?

Subcontractors know that you desperately need them in order to complete your project. If you refuse to pay market rate for your mats and subs, there is always a competitor who will. Value your suppliers and key relationships. Pay market rate for quality area subcontractors and popular inventory items; however, be responsible and set aside funds for these purchases. Reserve for the necessary cost right up front. Of course, take any opportunity you can to seek competitive bids for the service! Buy from the wholesaler with the lowest cost, but in the name of responsibility, let's reserve for this cost because we know it is a cost we must incur.

When estimating the amount to be reserved in mats and subs, I recommend looking at your historical cost. When you review your financial statements or your tax return, what percentage of your total sales typically goes toward mats and subs?

Analyze a few years. I love at least three years of comparative data. (See, my friend, how those financial statements are important?) What percentage of your total revenue, on average, is spent on your cost of goods sold? This average is the amount that you will allocate to your mats and subs. This is the TAP amount you will transfer to your Mats and Subs Account twice a month.

I already recommended that the Mats and Subs Account be a checking account. This way, you can pay for the purchase of inventory, materials, and subcontractors directly from the account. And you can monitor the status of this account to ensure that you are in line with your budget and are reserving enough as you go. In addition, I want you to feel the squeeze in the event that your mats and subs vendors are creeping their prices upward. If that happens, I need you to increase your sales price in proportion to the vendor price. If your vendors increase their prices by 3% annually, you will need to increase your price by a minimum of 3% annually in order to stabilize your profit impact.

PAY DOWN DEBT

As I WRITE THIS, OUR nation is going through a major transition. COVID-19 is here. Small Business Administration (SBA) loans are being issued in ways they never have before. Paycheck protection program loans, economic injury disaster loans, and other sources of seemingly "free" money are coming at business owners from the government in volumes we have never experienced before. MBE, it makes me nervous. I'm hoping that the majority of American business owners have a plan to pay down these loans.

One thing I am proud of is that, even though our nation has been hit with an economic recession and unemployment has exceeded 16%, my Profit First entrepreneur clients are still going strong. Throughout their time with me, these clients have reserved for moments like this, using their profits to build retained earnings and gradually pay down debt.

If you have debt, don't worry. I have a plan for you, too. I recommend an approach similar to the debt snowball method designed by Dave Ramsey, founder of Entreleadership, which I mentioned earlier, and Financial Peace University. Although created for personal finances, it works just as effectively in business.

On the 10th and 25th of each month, as part of your target allocation percentage (TAP) transfers, you will continue to transfer money into your Profit Account. This amount in this account will grow as a result of each transfer.

At the end of each quarter, I want you to review the balance that you have accumulated in your Profit Account. Take this accumulated amount and divide it in half. Yes, I said half. Then I want you to transfer the first half into another bank account, a bank account that is less accessible to you than your TAPs accounts. In fact, I recommend that you consider placing this money in a savings account at a local community bank. Better yet, a community bank that is rife with inconvenience and poor technology. Make it a place to which you have to drive, that requires planning if you're going to make the trip. Place half of your accumulated profit in this savings account, and label the account "The Vault."

When it comes to the other half, we will need to make some decisions. Do you have debt? If you do not have debt, congratulations! This half is all about you. Take it out, take it home, go on a dream vacation, buy that new car, put it in your 401(k), have fun with it! Celebrate. This money is all about you and whatever you want to do with it.

If you have debt, you are about to give yourself a gift that you will be proud of for generations to come. I want you to take that other half and make a payment on your smallest debt balance. When you make that payment, I want you to watch that balance go down. I want you to sit back with pride, knowing that you have taken the first step toward a debt-free business and life. Each quarter, I want you to do the same. Continue to pay off your smallest debt balance. Paying off the smallest debt balance first not only builds a solid debt management history, it also allows you to reduce the number of overall debt accounts on your balance sheet. When you pay off an account, put your money toward the next smallest balance. Do this successively until eventually you are *debt free*! Y'all feeling me! Our goal is to create debt-free businesses. You are going to forgo instant gratification for a solid, debt-free future.

Credit cards are tempting for small business owners. I find that they can easily get an entrepreneur into a vicious circle of debt. Some business owners really struggle with credit cards. In many ways, if not managed properly, credit cards can offset the Profit First experience. By using credit cards, you create an illusion of even bigger balances to play with; the opposite of the illusion of scarcity created by the small-plate Profit First approach. Plus, if you have a credit card balance that continues to increase, you will never be able to enjoy the fruits of your Profit Account.

I'd prefer that you don't maintain credit cards. I'd prefer you just paid for everything with checks. Unfortunately, that may not always be practical in this world. If you decide that you must maintain a credit card, you must also pay off the balance on the 10th and the 25th of the month, right before you pay any other bills. This way, you will feel that illusion of scarcity. Do not allow credit card balances to accumulate and sabotage your success.

My take on debt is that it is modern-day slavery. The Bible says, in Romans 13:8, NIV: "Let no debt remain outstanding, except the continuing debt to love one another, for whoever loves others has fulfilled the law." Proverbs 22:7, NIV, reads: "The rich rule over the poor, and the borrower is slave to the lender."

MBE, be no one's slave. Own your companies; live debt-free!

Those of us working to get there, to remove ourselves from bondage, use this debt snowball method to build equity and freedom.

NEXT STEPS

REVIEW YOUR YEAR-TO-DATE FINANCIAL STATEMENTS and identify opportunities for cost savings.

1. Export your P&L into Excel and sort your expenses from largest to smallest. For each expense, evaluate the return on investment for the payment.

2. If expenses do not offer an ROI, cut them.

3. Divide your Real Revenue by your total employee count (including the owner). Does this equate to at least

$150,000 generated for each employee? If not, is this an opportunity to increase prices or increase efficiencies?

4. If you have debt, let's start eradicating it. At the end of each quarter, take half of your profit and place it in the Vault Account. Use the other half to pay down your smallest debt.

Congratulations, MBE. You are on your way to running a wildly profitable, cash flow-positive business! Let's keep going! Onward!

CHAPTER NINE

Eat the Frog

AT THIS POINT, YOU ARE knee-deep in Profit First. You know all of the basics to thrive and build a successful minority business enterprise. You are ready to take over the world. You are ready to do great things, and you will do them profitably. Some of y'all, however, still haven't gone to the bank! This short chapter is for you.

You may have a thousand and one reasons why you have not set up your Profit First accounts yet. The hardest part is just getting started. Literally. It's sort of like anything worth accomplishing in life. When you are standing at the foot of the mountain, you think, "I will never make it to the top." However, once you have completed the mission, you find you are ready to climb an even larger mountain.

I love Mark Twain's comment about eating the frog. He said, "If it's your job to eat a frog, it's best to do it first thing in the morning. And if it's your job to eat two frogs, it's best to eat the biggest one first." Sometimes, in life, you just have to eat the frog. You just have to do it.

If you continue to do the same, you will continue to get the same results. The only way out is to do things differently. Start those bank accounts today. Make that 1% allocation. I know that some of you are thinking, *This is just too hard. My cash flow is tight. I don't know what to cut. I feel emotional and agitated all the time.*

I get it! I often feel emotional, and am not too fun to be around when I have to make some tough decisions.

However, for you, I say: Start with a small step. Make a small step. If you don't have financial statements because you have not yet contracted an accountant, take a look at your bank statements and especially that credit card statement. What expenses do you currently pay that you really just don't need? What expenses duplicate another expense? What can be done more efficiently? Did you find an erroneous expense? If so, I want you to call your vendor right now and cancel it.

I'll wait for a minute while you do it. Just do it.

Now, didn't that feel good? Even though it was an expense of only twenty dollars a month, you just saved yourself $240 a year! Feels nice, right? Go ahead and tackle another one. Let's see if we can cut $500 for the year! Easy, wasn't it?

Some of y'all may be thinking, *Okay, Susanne, that was easy, but there is no way I am going to make those target allocation percentages. I am just way too far away from this stage for it to happen. I need all my money right now.* Or you might be thinking, *I just don't know what to cut.* For you, I'd say, let's not start with expense cuts. Instead, grab your most recent P&L statement, if you have it. If you don't yet have financial statements, let's not get hung up. Grab your most recent tax return or bank statement. Based upon the reports you have, complete your Profit Assessment.

What percentage of your revenue went toward Owner's Compensation? What percentage of revenue went to your total Profit? Before starting Profit First, just about everyone paid taxes either out of Owner's Comp or Profit, so tax will most likely be zero for your current allocation percentage (CAP). How much did you pay yourself? This is your Owner's Compensation.

Now, all of the remaining deductions in your bank statement—if not transfers to other business accounts or payments to yourself—are most likely operating expenses. Total these up to find your operating expense CAP. What percentage of your revenue consists of the remaining operating expenses (OPEX)?

Operating Expense / Real Revenue = OPEX Current Allocation Percentage

Now that you have completed your Profit Assessment, you have reached your starting point. These are your CAPs. This is the foot of your mountain. It doesn't matter where you start; what's important is where you end up. Many people start from a disadvantaged background and rise way above it, and so can you! Lead. Become the example. Let's do this!

CHAPTER TEN

Build a Powerful Team

WHEN I WAS KID, I loved visiting with my friends. As I left the house and the door banged behind me, I could hear my mother shout 1 Corinthians 15:33, NIV: "Do not be misled: Bad company corrupts good character." Another of her favorite scriptures is Proverbs 13:20, NIV, "Walk with the wise and become wise, for a companion of fools suffers harm."

MBE: The company that you keep—the team you maintain—will become who you are.

When I think of an example of a corporation that went wrong due to the team members it chose, I think of the story of Denny's.

In 1993, Denny's was a wonderful restaurant. The food was delicious. When you wanted golden eggs, fluffy pancakes, and crispy hash browns, Denny's was the place the go. When you were on the road, there was no better comfort spot to make you feel at home. Many customers, all around the country, stopped for a break to dine at Denny's while traveling.

One day, twenty-one Secret Service agents covering President Clinton's speech at the U.S. Naval Academy stopped to dine at a Denny's in Annapolis, Maryland. The group was large, so they split up for seating purposes. The white Secret Service agents were quickly seated. Meanwhile, the six Black Secret Service agents continued to wait patiently for their table. Other customers who came into the restaurant after them, also white, were seated.

After some time, the Black Secret Service agents realized that this Denny's had no intention of serving them. It seemed that this location did not attend to Black people.

This event made national news. I mean *national*. For years, many, many people of color *refused* to dine at Denny's. Why, as a woman of color, would I choose to eat in a restaurant where I know I will not be served? Why waste my time? Why waste my money?

Denny's never had a written corporate policy that prohibited its employees from serving Black people. Nothing was ever written in the Denny's employee handbook listing races it would and would not serve. However, a single group of employees, at a single location in Maryland, made a significant decision for a national brand that would have a *national* impact for decades to come. In fact, the decision made by this group of employees not only cost Denny's its reputation, it also cost Denny's Corporation $50,000,000 in fines.

MBE, does your team reflect your values? Does your team represent you and everything you believe in? Is your team a team that you are proud of? As I mentioned in Chapter 8, studies show that one "A" player equals three "B" players, and three "B" players equal six "C" players. Hire well. If you hire only "A" players, you will lower your payroll cost. You will lower your cost because you will need fewer employees.

Take your time hiring. Don't make a hiring decision out of desperation or exhaustion. It is better to make do with fewer employees than have to later use a firehose to clean up the mess created by disastrous hires. *Hire well.*

KNOW YOUR VALUES

DEFINE YOUR VALUES BEFORE YOU hire. What is important to you? What does your company represent? What is your purpose? Consider: What can you just not tolerate? What are the characteristics that make you just want to walk away?

If the job you are hiring for requires specific skill sets from the beginning, test for those skill sets. Make your own test if one does not already exist on the market.

Our clients come to us from many different places. Some of these clients just ended a nightmare relationship with a previous accountant or bookkeeper. Our job is to clean up their accounting system and move them forward on the straight and narrow. In order for me to avoid seeing a hundred new onboarding clients or finding myself neck-high in new client messes, I need a strong team of problem-solvers.

Outside of integrity, my highest corporate value is for my team members to have the ability to solve problems. I require that my team members not take the easy way out. They cannot expect their supervisor to solve problems for them. Critical thinking skills are talents we salivate over here at Mariga CPA PLLC. To identify these special talents, we have created a special accounting test. This test has a huge problem-solving component built into it. We designed the worst of nightmares for an accountant, a broken balance sheet. This balance sheet is full of all sorts of errors. My team members are required to be true critical thinkers who can figure out a client's financial reality, identify what is broken in the current general ledger, fix it, and put the client on a system moving forward that will ensure they get accurate financial statements.

Spend time with your candidates. Take them out to lunch. Get to know them. Take them shopping, as Patrick Lencioni suggests in his book *The Ideal Team Player*.[10] Dave Ramsey, in his book *Entreleadership*,[11] writes that he actually takes his top candidates out to dinner and conducts interviews with their spouses. During a spousal interview, he not only finds out if he really likes the potential hire, he also ensures that the whole family is excited about the opportunity. Get to know your candidates well. The more time you spend with them, the more you wear down their defenses and get to know them as real people. Then you will know for sure if they are the best fit for your company.

I once interviewed several candidates for a secretarial position. This was a pretty high position in my company. The secretary would both represent me and my brand and interact with my clients. One of the interview requirements for applicants was that they create a presentation focused on what it is like to work in a public accounting firm. We did this because we knew that the secretarial position was not an easy one in which to be successful. In public accounting, there are

---

[10] Patrick Lencioni, The Ideal Team Player (San Francisco, CA: Jossey-Bass, 2016).

[11] Dave Ramsey, Entreleadership (Brentwood, TN: Howard Books, 2011).

always a lot of clients, a lot of deadlines, and a lot of moving parts.

The right person for this position was crucial. To figure out if I would like working with someone on a day-to-day basis, I took them to lunch with other members of the team. We purposely kept our internal conversations to a minimum because we welcomed awkward moments and wanted to see what the candidates would do. How would they respond to these moments of awkward silence? What questions would they ask? How would they share their thoughts? Boy, did we find out some things! Some of them were appropriate in a work setting. Some were just plain scary. We often learned about their families, their hobbies, their problems, and, sometimes, their tics and inappropriate behaviors. Allowing candidates to get comfortable with us helped them to get to know us better, too. And for a prized candidate, this was the very thing we needed to seal the deal. The interview lunch is still—usually—our deal-maker or deal-breaker.

Your people make up your company. Payroll is the largest expense on your income statement. Make sure every expense is an investment, your hires. Make sure they represent you well.

MIXING BUSINESS WITH PLEASURE

WHEN MY BUSINESS WAS ABOUT three years old and we were just starting to bring in our first employees, I began to get a lot of well-intended pressure from my family to hire my younger brother. Although he was a smart young man, he had run into an inopportune time in history. He happened to graduate from college when our nation was in an economic recession. Banks announced major defaults on their mortgage loans. Auto companies and insurance companies asked for bailouts. Talented young graduates with no experience could not find jobs because absolutely no one was hiring for entry-level positions. In fact, everyone was laying people off. At the time, we needed a more experienced person to join us. And my brother had no interest in working for his big sister. He wanted to make his own way in this world.

However, pressure from my family was intense. Every time they called me, it was to "check on the status" of my brother's application. Against my better judgment, I eventually caved.

I think we are naturally harder on our siblings. We want the best for them. We want to them to rise to the occasion. Sometimes, in our strict regimens and super high expectations for our next of kin, we can end up killing the very thing we were trying to foster. Taking continuous feedback from a big sister is tough for any little brother. We both agreed to part ways, and I am proud to say he has since built his own entrepreneurial ventures without the help of his big sister.

MBE, family-owned businesses are tough. Working with friends and family is much harder than working with those you don't know. Professional boundaries are often crossed just because of the very nature of the relationship. I recommend that, before you consider building a family-owned business, you also consider the gift you are giving someone when you allow them to make their own way in this world.

I got some really good advice from my church women's ministry leader, Misha Wooten: "If you would not hire this person if you didn't know them, don't hire them now just because they are in your immediate circle." Keep your head clear. Stick with the bigger vision. Align your actual circumstances with your long-term goals. When you hire quickly and for convenience, you will find that it is difficult to part ways and that you are often left to clean up a mess. Hire for your long-term goals. Align your actions with your ultimate business plan. Ignore the peer pressure.

REMEMBER: WE ALL START SOMEWHERE

IN MY EARLY YEARS OF managing people, my staff drove me nuts! I reviewed their work and wondered, *What in the heck was this person thinking? Isn't this common sense? Who makes this kind of mistake, other than someone who is careless?* Reviewing work became not only a disheartening experience, but also a real anger-fest. After all, the more mistakes my team member made, the less I could trust their work, and the less I could rely on them. The more time I spent reviewing or reworking their work, the more time I lost with my family. The more I had to clean up, the angrier I became. As a manager, I was overworked, underpaid, and really, really unhappy. It wasn't until later that I realized that my role as a manager was not just to manage people, but also to mentor them, to build them up into the professionals they would become.

Mentoring and building up your team is always easier when you hire the best. It is very difficult to teach work ethics and problem-solving habits. When rising in their careers, everyone will come to a point where their talent ends. Everyone will cross a bridge to a place where their work is no longer easy and they will just need to learn and do more. It will be easier for a team member to work through the hard times when they have strong problem-solving skills, grit, and the right work ethic.

When you hire people, even "A" players, you will need to invest your time and resources in building them up. Perfect employees do not come in a can. Everyone requires some amount of investment. So, when you hire, get yourself in the correct headspace and accept this fact. Accepting it early on will save you from a broken heart later.

The best way to train a talented employee is through continuous feedback. In our profession, we do something called review notes. In the review note process, when a staff member makes a mistake or there is a suggestion for improvement regarding the person's work, I write it down and create a list of revisions, suggestions, and feedback. I put this into a Word document, which I then email to the staff member.

The staff member is then required to respond to each review note in a different color font than the one I originally wrote it in. (I usually write the note in black ink, and the staff member usually responds in red.) The staff person is required to address every review note either with a correction to their work papers, if that is the appropriate course of action; a clarification on the project itself; or a response that the feedback has been noted and they will take it into account in the future.

The team member then emails the review note responses to me. At this point, I review the responses and, if the course of action taken by the staff person is appropriate, I will strike out the corresponding review note. If there is more work needed on the staff member's part, I will not strike out the note. Instead, I will request additional clarification in a third color, usually blue. I then return the document to the staff member, who is required to reclarify or correct, hopefully with the result that I can clear the review notes. If every point in the document has been stricken out, the project can move on to the next phase.

Although the first set or two of review notes issued to a new staff member is commonly painful for them, by the third project, the number of review notes issued will have drastically decreased. Not wanting to see fifty review notes again, this staff member will have learned from their mistakes. If I see recurring errors with various team members, I host a brief team meeting, letting everyone know about the trends I am seeing. I ask the team what they could do differently to prevent these errors from occurring. I then ask what plan of action is necessary to prevent these errors from occurring in the future.

If I continue to see the same review notes popping up with a team member, I address them in a face-to-face meeting to determine what the issues are and why they continue to occur. If the same review note continues to trend, I will document it in a write-up or performance review. If the pattern continues after a couple of warnings, I don't second-guess myself. This is now just insubordination, so I seriously consider letting go of the employee. Two rounds of review notes are typically all that is necessary to fix the problem, though. I rarely have to dismiss employees. Most want to do their best work and make the company look good. Hiring for ability is the responsibility of the hiring manager. *Hire well.*

MBE, this takes a lot of patience on the part of the manager. Teambuilding is an investment. It is an investment of time, energy, passion, and money. Choose your team members wisely. Choose employees who have the innate ability to do the job. A squad that possesses the ethics and grit to endure the learning process will make your company shine!

MBE, depending on your business, your review process may look different. If you own a restaurant, for example, it may look like giving gentle feedback to a new employee throughout the day. During this step-by-step process, you'll advise the employee and show them how to do things differently. You may want to do a feedback recap at the end of each week. To keep motivation high, you may want to fill the recap with positive observations in addition to recommendations for improvement.

When hiring, I like to look for employees who show that they have a little grit. Grit is that ability to take a setback, learn from it, and move even further based upon the experience. I can usually identify grit in a person through the lines of work they have been in before, or even from details of their situation in life. Did they work at a super busy restaurant? Did they stay at this restaurant for a long period of time? What were their biggest accomplishments and lessons learned in their previous job? Were they promoted often? Was their career on an upward trajectory? The stories I love are filled with setbacks. Candidates' responses to earlier setbacks predict how my they will deal with feedback and challenges. They are indicators of what I should expect from them in the future. It also tells me how creative they are at solving problems. I love out-of-the-box thinkers. MBE, look for grit in your candidates.

Spend the time it takes to mentor, acknowledge, and encourage your employees. Nothing is worse than watching the light in the eyes of a team member stop shining. To keep someone rejuvenated and hopeful of future opportunities, you will need to continuously acknowledge when you see a job well done. When you see behavior that you want replicated, acknowledge the good things, encourage your employees to keep going, and show them a career path within your company where they can grow and go to the next level. Don't let the light in the eyes of your employees go out. There is nothing worse than carrying a bunch of dead weight. If it happens, if someone finds that they are just no longer energized by the job, let them go. Counsel them to find their own happiness, and set them free. Don't keep the dead amongst the living. We all live our fullest lives when we live as we were intended to.

DO WORK THAT MATTERS

AT THE TIME OF THIS writing, a Black man by the name of George Floyd has just been murdered by police officer Derek Chauvin.

It was a senseless murder, filmed by a bystander's cell phone. George Floyd was unarmed and surrendered immediately, but was still forced by Chauvin on lie on the ground. Officer Derek Chauvin placed his knee on George Floyd's neck and leaned on it for eight minutes and forty-six seconds while smirking at onlookers. For over eight minutes, Mr. Floyd, pinned to the ground, called out to the officer for mercy. He screamed that he could not breathe. As he called out his dead mother's name, he died from asphyxiation. There were three other police officers present at the time of George Floyd's death. Each of these officers looked on without caring or attempting to stop the murder.

George Floyd, an African-American man, was murdered in front of all of America—in front of the entire world.

Our country is in mourning as I write this. A nationwide protest has continued for weeks, led by a movement called Black Lives Matter. Black Lives Matter is a movement against the violence inflicted on Black communities by police officers and vigilantes. The movement is so much bigger than this horrible event, however. It is the result of generations of mistreatment, abuse, and withholding the opportunity for equality in the pursuit of life, liberty, and happiness from African Americans.

When I first set out to write this book, I thought it would be a "know-how" book, an "each one, teach one" addition to the *Profit First* family of books. I now understand that my topic is so much bigger, so much more complex than a "know-how"-style book can communicate.

In 1919, a group of Black sharecroppers from Elaine, Arkansas were frustrated by the low wages they received in exchange for their hard work and labor. These sharecroppers knew that no matter how hard they worked under their current circumstances, they would not get anywhere.

On September 30, 1919, in an attempt to make a better life for themselves, they endeavored to form a union. A union would allow them to take home a larger share of the profits produced by their labor.

The sharecroppers' attempt to unionize was met with hostility from local law enforcement. The governor of Arkansas, Charles Brough, called for 500 armed soldiers to stop the sharecroppers' efforts. On October 2, 1919, more than 200 African-American sharecroppers, along with their wives and children, were murdered. They were murdered for wanting to provide a better life for their families. Murdered for wanting to change their legacies. This event is known as the Elaine massacre.[12]

I wish I could say that the Elaine massacre was an isolated incident. However, history is full of accounts and stories of Black people attempting to rise only to have their ankles cut by organizations such as the Ku Klux Klan and other white nationalist groups. I now understand the psychological impact and trauma that must first be overcome in order for us to move forward as a people.

When corporate America brags of diversity in their workforce, this diversity is typically in the lower echelon of their firms. There is heavy congregation of diversity within their mailrooms and secretarial staff. Very few corporate boards include members who are African American.

As small business owners, we have a unique opportunity to change the world. And as entrepreneurs, we have the ability to create a world where everyone, no matter their race, religion,

---

[12] Uenuma, Francine. "The Massacre of Black Sharecroppers That Led the Supreme Court to Curb the Racial Disparities of the Justice System." August 2, 2018. https://www.smithsonianmag.com/history/death-hundreds-elaine-massacre-led-supreme-court-take-major-step-toward-equal-justice-african-americans-180969863/

creed, gender, or sexual orientation, has the chance to compete for jobs. We have the power to grant others the opportunity to pursue life, liberty, and happiness. MBE, we have a calling and an obligation to lead this mission.

One of my greatest joys comes from looking at the careers of my past and present staff members. While I unhesitatingly admire the professionals they have become, I often remind myself that when they first started with me, many were just out of school and lacked professional experience. By the time they graduated from my firm, they had presented in front of large governmental boards, led substantial audit engagements, and gained the technical skills needed to outshine any member of a Big Four accounting team. I am fortunate that many of my staff members have been minorities. Although it has not been an easy task, I have helped create a conduit for them to be molded and developed into the leaders they are today.

Many of my staff members chose to work with a smaller accounting firm because they did not find a place at a larger, Big Four, majority-white accounting firm. Perhaps they were overlooked due to lack of experience or a lack of commonality with the interviewer. However, I was able to give them an opportunity with my firm. I would advise any business owner: If you desire to be a national brand in the 21st century, you will need to create a culture of inclusion. You will need to build a culture in which everyone feels welcomed, valued, and needed, in which everyone feels that their career holds limitless possibilities for their future.

The best way to do this is through mentorship. Feedback is critical, but encouragement and vision will go a lot farther. Get to know your team. These people represent you. These people are the face of your company. At some point, if you are really scaling, clients will know your team much better than they know you. Get to know what makes your people happy. What encourages them and makes their eyes light up? Why do they wake up every morning to serve your customers? Tell them often that they are doing a great job. Make everyone feel part of the team. Invite them to team lunches.

Share your story, and your vision. Everyone should be appreciated, regardless of their race, creed, color, or religion. If you do this, you will build a powerful team, successfully scale your business, and create a national brand.

CHAPTER ELEVEN

Enter New Rooms

KYM YANCEY IS THE LEGENDARY drummer from the R&B, soul, disco, funk, and Capitol Records gold album-winning band Sun. In his twenties, when Kym was not traveling with the band, he was busy growing his forty-person advertising empire. His original purpose for creating the advertising agency was to create a revenue stream for himself so that he could spend more time working on his array of music projects. However, he soon found that running a business takes up a lot of time. When I interviewed Kym for this book, he shared that, when you're growing a business you are passionate about, "It craves every ounce of creativity and every idea and insight that you have."

Early on in his business, Kym realized that there was a need for unique and captivating advertising in the auto sales industry. He would watch car dealers' advertising, and it was always the standard: a dealer would stand up in front of a car, or a lot full of them, and give the "I got the best prices, I got the best inventory" spiel. It was always the same old stuff.

Kym remembers a dealership in Dayton, Ohio called Peffley Ford. It was owned by a man named Peffley. Kym remembers calling Peffley on the phone and telling him, in essence, "You know, I'm from Dayton. I've seen your advertising, and you need a fresher approach. You need something that is going to stand out because you all are saying the same things all the time."

Peffley told Kym, "Do you have any idea how many people call me to tell me they've got better ideas? But here's what I'm going to do. I'm going to give you five minutes to show me what you've got." Peffley then scheduled an appointment with Kym for three months out.

Kym will never forget that. He recalled telling his wife later that night, "You know, I should probably cancel."

As the date of the presentation got closer and closer, Kym continued to contemplate canceling the appointment. Peffley was in his late sixties. Kym told me, "He looked like, you know, a good old boy. He seemed pretty gruff to me. And I thought, *I'm going to walk in there with this big Afro—this youth, you know— and I'm thinking he's going to prejudge me.* And I was playing all these tricks, mind games with myself about the reasons why maybe I should cancel."

Kym continued, "I didn't think we would be a good fit. And I think that's one of the things that entrepreneurs do too, you know, they talk themselves out of something. Well, here is the aha moment for me and I'm going to pass this one to everybody. I walked into that dealership and Peffley was sitting behind his desk and he had three or four of his other salespeople with him. They're all in polyester suits, and they're all standing with their arms crossed."

Kym told them, "I've put together a little jingle for you and some copy."

Kym then played them the jingle and shared a few other ideas.

Peffley said, "Young man, you got my business." He then looked at Kym as if he could sense his surprise. "You want to know why I'm giving you this account?"

Kym said, "Yeah, I'd love to hear this."

Peffley then shared, "The jingles are okay and your ideas are fine, but I want your enthusiasm. I want your excitement. You are so enthusiastic about my business and what I'm trying to do. I want that here, at this dealership."

"In other words," Kym explained, "he bought the excitement in my voice about his business and what he was trying to do. This was a real valuable early lesson for me. If you can't show that you're excited about something, if you can't show someone that you're excited about your idea, then no one is going to entrust you with their business. So many people try to be so cool and smooth that they fail to communicate the idea or their excitement about their idea. People buy positivity. People buy that excitement. They buy that energy, and that's not taught in any school or any program. That's part of life. It's part of that 'it' factor, that charisma that you bring to something. But that really taught me something. He wanted my excitement and desire to bring something new to his dealership. That's what he wanted, over and above the ideas I had given him."

MBE, no matter who you are pitching to, no matter your prospect's background, pitch your best with excitement. Let them turn you down! Don't rob yourself of an opportunity because of the "stuff" going on in your head.

MBE, if you are anything like me, it is outside of your comfort zone—outside of that which you know—where the opportunities lie. In this chapter, you'll learn how to navigate new opportunities within new peer circles. I'll teach you to go into rooms that you have never entered before, where people more than likely do not look like you.

THE NATIONAL MINORITY SUPPLIER DEVELOPMENT COUNCIL

WHILE WRITING THIS BOOK, I got the opportunity to interview Adrienne Trimble, CEO of the National Minority Supplier Development Council Inc. (NMSDC). Adrienne is a graduate of Wilberforce University, our nation's oldest private, historically Black university owned and operated by African Americans. She is known throughout the world for her thought leadership in the area of advancing corporate diversity, equity, and inclusion (DEI) initiatives.

The NMSDC minority business enterprise certification is the platinum standard in supplier diversity. NMSDC's certification verifies stability and recognizes promising minority business enterprises on behalf of its corporate members. These corporate buyers include many that rank within our nation's Fortune 500. NMSDC has more than 400 corporate members, including the likes of the Coca-Cola Company, Chevron Service Companies, ExxonMobil, and Abbott Laboratories. NMSDC's certification facilitates networking, allowing MBEs and corporate buyers to build long-lasting relationships.

Prior to her work with NMSDC, Adrienne served as general manager of diversity and inclusion at Toyota Motor North America. While at Toyota, Adrienne worked closely with the company's senior leadership team. There, she developed advocacy and accounting measures to integrate DEI processes across the organization's business operations. While in this role, Toyota rose from number forty-two to number twenty-five on the Diversity Inc. Top 50 list in just two short years. This elevation allowed Toyota to be recognized by third-party organizations such as Black Enterprise Best Companies for Diversity, Hispanic Association on Corporate Responsibility, and the United States Hispanic Chamber of Commerce.

Toyota has a strong belief in developing talent throughout different parts of the company. As a result, Adrienne received the opportunity to work in Toyota's procurement department, leading its supplier diversity initiative. The assignment was supposed to be for just two years, but it led to a career change for Adrienne. While leading Toyota's supplier diversity initiative, Adrienne found that her prior experience in the human resources side of business had laid the foundation for her understanding and commitment to diversity, equity, and inclusion (DEI). During her time in human resources, Adrienne recognized the importance of creating inclusive talent management strategies. These strategies are crucial throughout all areas of business, from recruitment to succession planning. She understood the necessity of ensuring that all people are included in hiring *and* procurement processes.

The importance of ensuring supplier diversity was personal to Adrienne not just because it allowed Toyota access to amazing talent, but also because of its impact on surrounding communities. Adrienne shared with me that minority business enterprises create jobs within their communities. Statistics show that minorities tend to hire other minorities at higher rates than non-minority companies do. This allows communities to become self-sufficient and sustainable. By creating stable jobs within underserved, underrepresented communities, discretionary and disposable income is generated within these communities. These communities then purchase from larger corporations, ultimately generating more corporate dollars.

When Adrienne saw the implications of the work of minority business enterprises and their creation of opportunities in underserved communities, it reminded her of the 1930s and 40s. When she thought about such communities and how strong they were during this era, she realized that they were more self-sufficient. These tight-knit communities had their own grocery stores, their own dry cleaners, and their own inherent economies. The dollars generated locally stayed within these communities, ultimately making them stronger.

When Adrienne thinks about the conflicts that exist in today's society, she sees that they are not about social issues so much as economic ones. To make sure that our U.S. economy is strong, we have to ensure that businesses are successful.

When Adrienne looks at minority business enterprises that have really grown to scale, the common denominator she identifies is that they have true business champions within their customers' supply chains. These champions help MBEs navigate the corporate footprint and understand how they can grow and connect them to end buyers and key decision-makers within their own organizations. MBEs, in turn, understand their customers' problems and know how to deliver the solutions. They know what their customers are looking for, and they bring the right solutions to the table.

Often, when MBEs lack a connection inside a company who is willing to mentor them or provide them with an understanding of the company's culture, sourcing strategies, and what's important to them as a business, MBEs are unprepared to provide necessary solutions. So, when Adrienne sees minority business enterprises that have really been able to grow and scale, it's those that have developed deep relationships with their customers and possess the ability to not only meet but also anticipate their needs. MBEs who know their customers bring the right solution at just the right time.

One of the things NMSDC does best is to connect minority businesses with corporate supply chain decision-makers. This allows MBEs to develop those important relationships. Adrienne advises us that in any type of business, people do business with people that they know, like, and trust. These relationships don't form overnight. There has to be a means for these individuals to get to know each other in an informal setting. For example, when folks are playing golf, they typically meet at a country club. If MBEs don't show up in such circles, they miss out on opportunities to learn some crucial, informal information, such as details about corporate supply chain needs. This kind of information is important for an MBE to access in order to be successful in corporate America.

Adrienne explains that the way to get that kind of access is by working through organizations like NMSDC and its affiliate councils, which provide opportunities to meet the buyers, the key decision-makers, and the operations people who are looking for business solutions. The people you meet while part of NMSDC will provide meaningful information as to how you can actually solve some of the problems facing their companies.

WHEN YOU ARE THE ONLY ONE IN THE ROOM WHO LOOKS LIKE YOU

As your business progresses, you will come to a point where you frequently enter crowded rooms in which no one else looks like you. When I observe a career like that of Adrienne Trimble, I can't help but imagine the rooms she must have walked into.

When I interviewed Adrienne for this book, I had to ask, "Rising through the ranks of corporate America, you probably found that you were the only African American in the room. I know that as MBEs, we often suffer from 'imposter syndrome,' that feeling that occurs when no one in the room looks like us except the waitstaff and the janitorial crew. How do you navigate rooms such as these, and have the courage to meet decision-makers?"

Adrienne said, "I can only speak for me and what's been helpful for me, and how I helped others come into the room. First of all, I think it's incumbent upon those of us who get into those roles to help bring others into the room. That's a responsibility that we should own, and be willing to open those doors for others because someone had to open the door for us. So, in my opinion, that's the way you get comfortable, first of all. If you are invited into that room, then you belong in the room. So, you act like you belong in the room and you own it. You make sure that you take advantage of being in that world.

"For me, it's really making sure that once that door is open, you get in and you make sure that you get the right information you need to be able to grow your business. It's going to help your business, but also keep the door open for the next person to come through. That's how we get stronger as a minority business community. We make sure that we're helping others get to the same position that we're trying to get to."

When I asked Adrienne the question, "If you could offer one piece of advice to the next up-and-coming, rising MBE, what would it be?" she replied: "Reach out and get a mentor. There are so many successful MBEs that want to share their knowledge, their wisdom, and their lessons learned with the next generation. They want to make it just a little bit easier than maybe they had to have. Don't be afraid to reach out and ask some of those folks. If you see someone that's had success with a customer that you're targeting, ask them what lessons they can share with you so that you, too, can achieve those levels of success. Don't be afraid to make the ask and to get that type of information."

Adrienne's answer didn't surprise me. It confirmed the reality. MBE, own the room and leave the door open for another to have the same opportunity.

NETWORKING

Kym Yancey, whom I introduced earlier in this chapter, is now the Co-founder and president of eWomenNetwork. Kym realized long ago that while entrepreneurs need to prospect with major corporations, they often lack the access to reach the key decision-makers. This understanding led him and his wife, Sandra Yancey, to establish a network that helps women (and also men) get connected to the market and promote their businesses.

When I asked Kym about his early career, prior to eWomenNetwork, he shared, "I never liked going to networking events. I always felt like I lost. I went there wanting to talk but had to let them talk. And I'm thinking in my mind, *Well, are you about finished so I can tell you about me?*"

Kym confessed, "I didn't understand the principles, no one had shared with me what networking was all about. My friend George Fraser, out of Cleveland, is brilliant. He's a bestselling author. He's incredible. I'll never forget that during my ad agency days, I went to his book signing in Dayton. He had a book out called *Success Runs in Our Race*. Powerful. I had heard about him, but I had never met him. It was the middle of the afternoon. There were probably ten or twelve people in the store milling around. I stood up the entire time to watch George. And he says, 'First of all, let me explain to you what networking is. Networking is not about getting; it's all about giving. When you network to give, you always feel energized, you always feel happy to be involved in meeting people because you're looking for ways to give to them. You're taking the pressure off *you* to get something, and that reciprocity is universal law. When you give to others, people want to do the same thing for you. Now, you don't give thinking that I'm giving to you because I expect something back. You give authentically because you want to help. Through that, it just naturally happens for you.'"

Kym then shared, "That changed everything for me. I realized that a whole lot of that awkwardness I had felt was in my own head. I had conjured up in my own thinking what people thought of me or whatever the case may be. But that whole thing of the games we play on ourselves, of what we think, and how we think people are perceiving us and receiving us and understanding us, we can think our way out of an opportunity. That Peffley Ford situation and that meeting, that networking chance with George Fraser, just changed the trajectory of my life."

On September 18, 2020, eWomenNetwork celebrated its twentieth anniversary. Kym Yancey not only mastered the art of networking; he also created a platform to allow other entrepreneurs to connect and thrive. MBE, networking is about giving and improving the life of others. As universal law has it, when it's your time to receive, you most definitely will.

BUILD A NETWORK OF POWER PLAYERS

THE BIGGEST LESSON I'VE LEARNED in business along the way—the least expected and the least spoken of—is this: Birds of a feather flock together. MBE, as Jim Rohn famously said, "You are the average of the five people you spend the most time with." If the five people you hang around with are movers and shakers, you are most likely a mover and shaker. If the five people you hang around with just never seem to get anywhere, this may be why you struggle to meet your goals. People are attracted to people who are heading in the same direction!

I love the book *The Proximity Principle* by Ken Coleman. In this book, Ken illustrates the power of association and how doors can be opened for you because of it. Ken states that "The right people + the right place = opportunities."[13]

MBE, who are the five people you spend the most time around every day, who have the most influence on your life? Peel back a layer. How do these top five people influence your life? Do they propel you forward, or are you constantly swimming against the tide? Are you leading these people, or are they leading you? You are most likely the average of these five people.

At the start of this chapter, I shared some of the Bible quotes my mother said to me whenever I left the house. As you may recall, her favorite thing to say to me as I went out the door to see my friends was from 1 Corinthians 15:33, NIV: "Bad association corrupts good character." She wanted to protect me as a young teen. Her well-meaning effort to guilt me was to ensure that the friends I chose to be with influenced me in the right direction. She wanted to make sure that I moved in the right way, that I stayed out of trouble.

For adults, the same advice holds true. We are the average of the five people we hang around with.

When I first started my business, the first piece of advice someone gave me was that I should join the local chamber of

---

[13] Ken Coleman, *The Proximity Principle* (Mahwah, NJ: Ramsey Press, 2019), 14.

commerce. This person bragged that the chamber of commerce was the place to go to find my buyers, the movers and shakers. Innocently, I followed this well-intended advice. I spent my last $300 on the membership.

When I joined the chamber of commerce, the first thing they told me was that I needed to get involved. I needed to join a committee. I needed to make sure everyone knew who I was. They hosted a ribbon-cutting event for me. They were nice people.

Based upon a recommendation, I joined the chamber's networking event, held every Wednesday morning at seven a.m. I was a new mother at that time, so attending meant that I had to hire a babysitter who was willing to arrive by six a.m. so I could get to the networking event on time. Before I walked out the door, I had to make sure that Florence, my baby, had all the supplies she needed. I also needed to make sure I presented myself well at the meeting. So, in order to have adequate preparation time, I had to wake up at five a.m.

When I arrived at the chamber networking event, I met many cheerful people who were quick to hand me their business cards and invite me to sit. Although the members were friendly, something just did not feel right. They never stopped talking about the products or services they were selling, and asking me if I knew of someone who might want to buy from them. They rarely asked me about my interests or what I was doing and, frankly, did not even seem to care. Deep down, it felt as if I was just wasting my time.

After of couple of weeks of waking up at five a.m. for this, I acknowledged my intuition and came to the conviction that I was indeed just wasting my time. You see, there were no business owners in the room. Everyone who attended the seven a.m. networking meeting was a business development professional. These were salespeople trying to make their monthly quotas. The plain truth was that they just did not need my services.

I am a business tax accountant. Although I could do personal returns, this was not the area I wanted to focus on. The people in attendance were not entrepreneurs. They did not own businesses and had no reason to hire a business tax accountant. Although they promised that they would refer me to others who did, their promises seemed empty. They were focused on their own quotas. On the off chance that one day, one of their clients just happened to ask if they knew an accountant, I am sure they would have thought of me, but what was the likelihood of this ever happening?

One of the best things I ever did was to stop attending those seven a.m. meetings. I cherish being able to sleep for an extra two hours. MBE, don't waste your time spinning your wheels in situations that will not lead to your desired outcome. Get out! Get out quickly! Pass go and do not stop until you hit your desired destination!

Although my friend's advice was well-intended, it was the biggest waste of good money and time ever. I am not advising you, MBE, not to join your local chamber of commerce. I think that there can be good value in a chamber. I am just recommending that you analyze your expenses. Ensure you are spending your time in places and with people that will drive you forward, toward to your desired outcome.

Be willing to shake hands, get to know new people, and enter circles where people don't look like you. Embrace those who seem outwardly to have nothing in common with you. This was a hard lesson for me learn. I wish I had learned it earlier.

I grew up in Cincinnati, Ohio, in a neighborhood called Seven Hills. I attended Mount Healthy high school, a predominantly African-American school. I was made fun of every day because of my race. I am half Chinese and half Black. Very few Asians went to my school, and very few biracial children attended in those days. Every day, I was reminded that I was different. I was considered too smart, too Chinese. My classmates clearly let me know that I did not belong, something I still find offensive to this day.

Unfortunately, young children from disadvantaged backgrounds often think too narrowly. This is especially true when they are succumbing to peer pressure while embracing a televised culture. Television, sadly, often stunts one's ability to thrive beyond the limits of one's neighborhood. I pray that, one day, all children can learn a new definition of "cool."

Looking back, I think that my parents should probably have placed me in a different school, a school attended by academically talented kids. However, my parents had five kids. They were stretched thin on time, and money was not an abundant resource. They could not hire a nanny. So school became a game of survival, one I had to just get through, filled with days that I wished would end.

Based upon my scholastic background and those with whom I attended school, I was unused to working around those who were not people of color. My mother had grown up in the South, my grandfather was a sharecropper, and his mother's mother was just one generation removed from slavery. Growing up, I heard many stories from my family about the mistreatment and trauma that my mother, grandfather, and great-grandmother had experienced at the hands of white people. These were stories about why I should not trust white people, how to limit my interactions with them, and how to just plain avoid them. Now imagine me coming into the real world, where I had to work with them and trust them. A lot of these white people would eventually affect my career and determine, as a young woman, where it would go. Imagine the stress involved with that!

Luckily, there are good people on both sides of the fence. There are good Black people, good Asian people, good Latino people, and good white people. At the same time, some bad people exist among all races. If I take this thought a little deeper, I acknowledge that there is probably both good and bad within all of us. We just choose what we will do and who we will become.

In this century, to build a national brand, you must cultivate a culture of inclusivity. You must create a culture in which everyone, regardless of their skin color, creed, nationality, race, religion, gender, or sexual orientation, feels welcomed, valued, and needed. You must create an environment in which everyone can feel hopeful about their own future opportunities. This means that you will need to reach across party and racial lines. You will need to shake hands with and embrace those who don't look like you.

If you have come from a background similar to mine, this will be uncomfortable at times. It will be scary. It will mean moving to a new level.

I have been attending Dave Ramsey's Entreleadership conferences for several years now. I love these conferences. The guest speakers are the best. The materials are amazing. I learn many things. Unfortunately, at any given conference, there are just a few handfuls of Blacks or people of any minority race in the room except for the waitstaff and hotel team. Hundreds of people attend these events, so the lack of diversity just feels weird. I don't think Dave Ramsey and his team are racist; I think that the cost to attend these conferences is a hefty investment and that MBEs choose not to pay the price. They don't correlate the investment with a return. They choose not to invest in themselves at that level.

Sometimes, to up-level your game, up-level your association and enter new rooms, you have to be willing to invest in yourself. Now, I am not saying that minorities can't up-level their game among other minorities. I am saying that there is talent outside of our inner circles. Sometimes, by tapping into the ideas and potential of others, we can bring them into our own circles.

Due to my background, neighborhood, and primary and secondary environments, I was not naturally connected with a lot of movers, shakers, and thought leaders. For the most part, I built this network on my own. At some point, I found that I just didn't have a lot in common with those I naturally hung around with; we didn't have much to talk about except for our kids, the weather, and our latest hobbies. I was building a business that I intended to scale; my natural associates were stay-at-home moms or lower-level employees of large corporations. They could not understand my challenges when it came to managing people, trying to get higher-paying customers, or balancing being a mother with moving into an executive-level role. They saw my stretching and dreams as me chasing the wind and never being satisfied. Some also felt that I looked down on them. I believe that this was a reflection of their own internal state, a lack of self-esteem and ability to see their own self-worth.

At some point, MBE, you may grow out of your inner circle. You will need to expand that inner circle. Sometimes the people who start the race with you will not be the people who finish it with you. Sometimes you will need to redefine who you are and create a bigger circle.

For me, growing my circle meant joining organizations of people who were moving in the same direction I was going. My organizational memberships changed over time. I started with my local minority business council when I first began my firm because I needed to see how contracts were won. The influence of other minority entrepreneurs gave me a greater vision of what I could become in and with my own company.

Later, I needed more in-depth help with the human resource side of my business. (Yes, I had managed people before starting my own company, but when you are scaling a company, you often grow out of previous roles.) This is when I joined Dave Ramsey's Entreleadership Program. In it, I was mentored weekly by Chris Oakley and the Entreleadership team. This experience taught me to lead people and establish boundaries to protect myself and my company in anticipation of where we needed to go.

At some point, I just got tired of seeing the entrepreneurs who came to me for tax preparation drown in accumulated business losses and compounding debt. This is when I joined the Profit First Professionals. I wanted to join the mission of eradicating entrepreneurial poverty. Today, I am writing this book in partnership with bestselling author Mike Michalowicz.

To get where you are going, to go beyond where you started, you will need to do new things. You will need to enter new circles. Do not be afraid. Do not hesitate. Do not hold yourself back.

Along the way, you may enter rooms that just don't feel right. Rooms where folks are just not friendly. MBE, always be kind, assess the situation quickly, and, if necessary, go find another room. Only stay in rooms where you will grow and be your best. I've discovered that many times, when people mistreat me or seem unfriendly, it really isn't about me. Deep down, it is really their own issue. Perhaps they are insecure. Perhaps they have never been taught to be charming and friendly to others. Maybe they are just plain shy or scared. They need to feel safe, and have not yet grown out of their own inner circle. Embrace who you are. If you find you are wasting time in a room, go to another room. Move on from rooms that don't allow you to grow.

Some of the rooms you enter will be in educational or professional development settings. Some of these rooms, especially the powerful ones, will have hefty fees associated with them. Always consider your return on investment. Can you gain access to these lessons in a less expensive way? Will you gain access to the brainpower of thought leaders if you do not enter this room? Consider your alternatives, but whatever you do, do not hold yourself back. Enter the room.

CHAPTER TWELVE

Increase Profits Through Tax Strategies

BILLIONAIRE INVESTOR WARREN BUFFET BRAGS that he pays taxes in a lower bracket than his secretary does. In this chapter, I will tell you how he does it.

I meet too many business owners who are hyper-focused on driving down their taxable income by increasing expenses. These entrepreneurs shortchange themselves before they even begin. They brag that they would rather buy another $40,000 truck than pay taxes to the government, but as they ramble on at me in my office about their schemes to undercut the government, I can't help but think, *So you would rather spend $40,000 on something you don't need just to save $10,000 on taxes?* Wouldn't it be better to save that $40,000 and invest in a new piece of rental property or, better yet, put the money away in an investment account for their child's future college education?

Today, MBE, I challenge you to think bigger. How can you use tax strategy to reduce taxes while *avoiding* expense increases? Better still, how can you *defer* taxes so that you are not taxed today, but rather in the future, when you can always control how and when you draw out the money? How can you delay taxation to a time when you can create an artificially lower tax bracket? I want you to think about how you can use tax strategy to achieve both your business and personal financial goals.

LET'S TALK CORPORATE ENTITY SELECTION

ACCOUNTANTS OFTEN TELL THEIR CLIENTS to form an S corporation entity as soon as they start a business. I love S-corps as much as the next accountant. They are amazing because they allow you to avoid the double taxation required of traditional C corporations (S-corp earnings flow through the owner's personal tax return on a form K-1). And S-corps are fabulous because, as of this writing, they allow you to take a qualified business income (QBI) deduction of 20%. However, an S-corp is not always the best answer.

For example, if you require a lot of capital to start a business, an S-corporation may not be the best option for you. If you are the owner of a new manufacturing facility, much of your new business has been financed with debt, and your company is running at a loss, as an S Corp, you will not be able to deduct for the losses or offset the losses with income on your personal tax return. This is because you will be limited by something called basis when you do not have enough equity in your business for the IRS to allow you to deduct the loss. The IRS does not want you running companies at a loss. The government does not want you knee-deep in debt, so they have created tax laws to discourage you from running businesses that lose money. The IRS does not win when you lose money, and you don't win when you lose money.

If you are the owner of a start-up company that requires a large capital infusion to get going and you know that your business will initially be funded by debt, then perhaps you should consider forming your business as a single member LLC, taxed as a sole proprietor on a schedule C. By electing to be treated as a disregarded entity, you will be able to offset losses with other income, such as income from another company that you own, a separate W-2 from a wage-earning job, or perhaps even your spouse's earnings. Choosing single member LLC status means that your opportunities to offset losses with other income will not be wasted. Nor will you be trapped in a cycle of carrying losses forward into future years where, hopefully, your performance will improve. If, in the first year of operations, you hit it out of the ballpark with your new company and end up making a profit—because, heck, you did just pick up this book—your accountant can always file a late election for your business to become an S corporation.

When choosing a business entity, you must also consider your long-term and short-term goals. If you have a thriving minority business enterprise now because you have implemented Profit First, you may find yourself entering into a realm where your income level now prohibits you from taking some of the tax deductions and financial benefits that you once enjoyed. At the time of this writing, the U.S. corporate tax bracket has never been lower. At 21%, the corporate tax bracket is below the average American individual income tax bracket.

If your business is formed as a C corporation, you may take a reasonable salary for the work that you do. And if you delay distribution of your earnings to avoid double taxation, you can create an artificially lower personal tax bracket. This means that you can reduce your overall taxes paid. In addition, your lowered income may qualify you to participate in programs such as an Individual Retirement Account (IRA) or a Coverdell education savings account (Coverdell ESA). These are programs that you may previously have been ineligible for due to your higher income level.

Tax law is complex. I definitely recommend that you work with your accountant instead of going it alone. You will also need to watch for changes in corporate tax rates. Changes do happen from time to time as political parties gain or lose power.

One of my favorite tax strategies, one I wish more Americans considered, is creating tax deferral strategies. On April 15th, many accountants will tell their clients, "Go out and put your money into an IRA." These CPAs will recommend the traditional pretax IRA and, for those who are in a lower tax bracket, they may encourage a Roth IRA. These are great entry-level accountant strategies.

I am going to challenge you, MBE. I want you think like Warren Buffet. I want you to think like the MBE you really are. How can you put away more than the measly $6,000-or-so IRA contribution? How can you have a tax reduction while still keeping the money? You can just keep kicking the can of tax burden toward another day, a day like retirement, when you can always control the amount of money you draw out of your retirement savings. Yes, at some point you will have to deal with IRS mandated minimum required distributions dispersed from your retirement accounts, but these will probably be way less than you are making now, especially if you are using the Profit First cash management method.

Consider contributing to a 401(k) plan. In 2021, the maximum contribution you can make for yourself, via combined employee and employer contributions, is $58,000 a year. I imagine that this contribution limit will only go up. After all, the government is currently stuck in the dilemma of determining how they will continue to fund Medicare and Social Security. Eventually, the straw will break, and we may one day be required to fund our own retirements. Wouldn't strategically putting away $58,000 for your own retirement be awesome for your tax savings? Your tax bracket will determine how much you actually save, but if you are amongst our nation's wealthiest, with a tax rate of 37%, this can be an annual savings of $21,460 a year.

You will need to be careful, however. The Employee Retirement Income Security Act (ERISA) laws are strict. What you do for yourself, as an employer, you will also need to do for your employees. Even so, there are ways around that; there are plans that allow you to maximize your own personal contributions! Like I said, there are loopholes for everything. Again, it is important to partner with a tax accountant who works with high net worth-clients. Align with an CPA who is appropriate for the current leg in your business journey.

One of the plans I love is the Qualified Automatic Contribution Arrangement (QACA). With the QACA, you are required to auto-enroll all of your eligible employees at a minimum determined contribution rate. At this point, your employees may elect to opt out of the plan. MBE, please encourage your employees to stay enrolled. Retirement is something that we all have to think about, plan for, and prepare to fund on our own. The sooner you start saving, the more you will accumulate. Encourage your team to save too. One of the best things you can do for them is help them plan for retirement. You will not regret advising someone to act in their own best interest.

The great thing about the QACA is, if your employees choose to opt out, you do not have to provide an employer match for them. I also encourage entrepreneurs to consider implementing a profit share plan within their 401(k) plans. This allows them to allocate additional contributions toward their 401(k)s, thereby reducing their taxable income. Y'all hearing me? Put money away. Defer taxation to another day. The 401(k)-profit share contribution is the way to go for my high earners.

Now I want you to consider your company values. What is your vision for your company? What are the areas in which you want to see improvement? What are some other ways of increasing profitability?

My thoughts go toward reducing turnover. If I can recruit "A" level employees, train them, invest in them, and better yet *retain* them, need I say that this is pure gold? It is said that it costs a company somewhere between six and nine months of an employee's salary to replace that team member. If you can retain your "A" players, you are, in effect, increasing profitability because you are keeping a good thing going.

I recommend creating initiatives that encourage employee longevity. Build your values into your 401(k) plan. In the 401(k) world, we refer to this as a vesting strategy. Select the longest vesting period that you legally can. In this case, though your employee receives employer matching contributions, the employee is not fully vested in the plan until they have been with you for a set number of years. Currently, this vesting period for the QACA employer matching contribution is a maximum of two years. However, for the profit share 401(k) contributions, the maximum vesting period is six years. Wouldn't it be nice to retain your "A" players for at least six years? Imagine the productivity you will reap from these employees.

Also, offering employee benefits at this level will place you way ahead of most of your competition. Many of your competitors are only attracting talent based upon salary. You, on the other hand, are incentivizing your employment opportunities with your lovely 401(k) plans. Even more interesting, you are competing against the big corporations on an even playing field. Now I am impressed because you're using some serious tax strategy!

Here is the kicker, MBE: Remember that I said I wanted you to think like Warren Buffet. Let's say that lovely "A" player has turned out not to be the loyal sidekick you always wanted, and the pretty lights of a competitor have drawn them away. Let's assume that they left before fully vesting in your lovely, gracious, and generous contributions. That "A" player says, "Love ya! I'm out of here." Well, guess what? Although the employee is fully vested in their own personal contributions and will take those with them, if your employer contributions are not fully vested, those funds go back into the plan! Then you, as the plan owner, can choose to allow those forfeited funds to either be used as future matching contributions for other employees, or to allow those funds to sit unused in the retirement fund until the end of the life of the company. In the latter case, unused 401(k) money would remain invested until the moment you choose to dissolve the company. At that point, the money just goes to the remaining employee. Which is whom, by the way? If you are strategic, it can be you! Now, are you hearing me? Tax strategy, MBE.

You sole-employee, owner-operators out there are even luckier. You are lucky because you don't have to worry about matching employee contributions. This money is all yours. Your only restrictions are the ERISA contribution limits! Keogh plans are amazing for single owner-operated business entities. Just about all brokerage firms have a Keogh plan available for single-member LLCs or sole proprietors. These plans are usually simple to start, and the paperwork can be completed within two hours. The tax savings are definitely worth exploring. MBE, in this situation, you create a deduction without spending money; you get a deduction for pay you will receive in the future, when you *one* day retire.

Current capital gains rates are amazing. Capital gains rates apply when you hold an investment for at least a year prior to selling the investment. When you sell these investments at a price greater than the price at which you purchased them, capital gains rates apply. This tax treatment also applies to qualified dividends. And this is how Warren Buffet pays taxes in a lower bracket than his secretary does. I bet the majority of his income comes in the form of capital gains and dividends. After all, Warren Buffet is known for his strategic investments! For married filing jointly taxpayers, the capital gains rate is zero for those with income under $80,000, 15% for those with income between $80,001 and $496,600, and 20% for those with income greater than $496,601. Can you imagine earning $80,000 and paying zero taxes on your investment income? Even in a higher tax bracket, you can pay taxes at a much lower rate—20% instead of 35%. This is a 15% tax savings for those earning $501,600!

The 2021 traditional tax brackets for married filing jointly are as follows:

Married Filing Jointly Income Level	Tax Bracket	Capital Gains Rate
$0 to $19,900	10%	0%
$19,901 to $81,050	12%	0% up to $80,800, then 15%
$80,051 to $172,750	22%	15%
$172,751 to $329,850	24%	15%
$329,851 to $418,850	32%	15%
$418,851 to $628,300	35%	15% up to $501,600, then 20%
$628,301 and over	37%	20%

As you can see, MBE, although your normal tax bracket is only 12% with an income of less than $81,050, if this same income were produced by capital gains transactions, you would actually be taxed at 0%. Imagine making money and legally not paying any taxes. This is pretty cool, isn't it? Take advantage of capital gains tax rates! Lower your taxes!

Please note, MBE, I am not giving investment advice. You will need to speak to your investment manager to determine the best investment strategy for *you* before taking any action. As you begin to build your wealth using the Profit First method, you might consider shifting your money into qualified dividend-yielding investments. That way, you will not only be able to replace your normal income in the long-term; you will also be able to replace it with income taxed at the rate of a lower tax bracket.

Now you are thinking like Warren Buffet. Build profitability and wealth through tax strategy.

INCOME SHIFTING

ANOTHER REALLY COOL STRATEGY IN tax planning is income shifting. Income shifting occurs when you take income from a person who is currently in a high tax bracket, which often occurs in Profit First clients, and then shift the income to someone of a lower tax bracket. Hiring your children and giving them a meaningful work experience is a great way to do this. My dad hired me when I was fourteen. I was the bookkeeper in his accounting firm. I learned how to make journal entries and reconcile bank accounts within his accounting system. I learned the difference between debits and credits and even how to balance the books, a skill that I often teach my new college grads today when they start work in my own accounting firm.

Malcolm Gladwell, in his book *Outliers*,[14] says that it takes 10,000 hours to become an expert. 10,000 hours equal ten years of experience. So, technically, I became an accounting expert by the time I was twenty-four, just when my peers were

---

[14] Malcolm Gladwell, Outliers (New York, NY: Back Bay Books, 2011).

graduating from college. I chuckle when I think of this. I passed my CPA exam on the first try. Only 4% of examinees were able to accomplish that in 1999, but that is what happens when you start at fourteen.

MBE, if it takes 10,000 hours to become an expert, imagine what would happen if you gave your children the gift of apprenticeship. Imagine if you were able to pass your own skill sets down to your children and give them not only skills to carry with them and hopefully pass on to future generations, but also a competitive advantage over their professional peers. Plus, guess what else you get? A tax deduction. Hiring your children, paying them a fair wage for a fair day's work, and giving them a new skill for life is pretty great. And in return, you get a tax deduction for shifting your tax rate to that of your children. If you hadn't hired your children, this money would have been income, taxed according to your higher tax bracket. However, because your children are now earning this money, it is taxed at a much lower rate corresponding to their tax bracket—unless your children are Bitcoin geniuses, that is!

If your children earn less than the standard deduction, guess what? They are not required to file a tax return and their federal tax rate is 0%. So now you have shifted your own income from, let's say, your high net worth tax bracket of 37% into your child's low tax bracket of 0%. Now you can require little Suzie or little Tommie to pay for their own extracurricular activities. You earned a write-off from paying your child to learn a skill that just happens to help you in your business, and now your child can sponsor their own hobbies.

Even better, you can require that your child invest their money in a Roth IRA. A Roth IRA is an after-tax retirement account. When your child is in the 0% federal tax bracket because they have earned less than the standard deduction, and they place their after-tax (0% tax bracket) earnings into a Roth IRA, they can draw out that money tax-free at retirement. Your child can also use the money accumulated in their Roth IRA account to pay for college tax-free and penalty-free.

Depending on your entity election, there may be some Social Security, Medicare, and state taxes due from your child's income; overall, though, it is likely that your child is in a lower bracket than you are.

REAL ESTATE

REAL ESTATE IS ANOTHER GREAT investment strategy. My husband, Jeff, loves owning rental property. It allows him to dabble a little in the business world while building his net worth in a way that requires very little effort on his part. He does a little heavy lifting when he first purchases properties, but after a property is set up, it is smooth sailing.

When Jeff first started investing, I was really concerned that we would get odd calls from renters throughout the night, but it has not been that bad. His rental property business practically runs itself. He signs long-term leases with his tenants, which he incentivizes by offering small discounts if they sign multi-year leases. Jeff also places his tenants on autopay. Now he no longer chases them for rent checks each month. Brilliant! Did I tell you my husband is a pretty smart guy? It's quite the passive business.

Jeff has a double benefit, besides marrying an accountant: First, all of the income he earns from his rental properties is recorded on a Schedule E in his tax return. As a Schedule E venture, it is a passive activity for him. Here is the second benefit, and the interesting part! The money he earns from his rental business is not subject to self-employment taxes. Jeff does not have to contribute to Social Security, Medicare, or employer taxes on earnings from his rental property business. This is a tax savings of up to 15.3%. Passive income is a beautiful thing. You will want to speak with your accountant to make sure your business qualifies as passive activity. Each situation is unique.

Owning real estate is one of the best ways to accumulate wealth. In most areas of the United States, real estate tends to hold its value. Once you own your home free and clear, you can live rent-free for the remainder of your life. If, after living in your home for two years, you sell that home within a five-year period (which includes the two years that you lived in the home), any earnings or gains you make on the sale of the home are tax-free (as long as these gains are within certain limits). If you buy a home for $200,000, live in the home for two years, and sell it for $300,000 within the next three years, that additional $100,000 you earned is a tax-free transaction. You can exclude up to $250,000 of gain associated with the sale of your home if you are single and live in the home for two years, and up to $500,000 of gain if you are married filing jointly. The rules can get more complicated than this. Before implementing any of these strategies, I recommend that you reach out to your accountant.

Let's have a little more fun. Let's say now that Tommie doesn't need to touch his Roth IRA. He is an amazing chess player (got it from his momma, I heard!) and he's got scholarships, so he doesn't need any additional money for college. When Tommie wants to buy his first house, he can actually take a distribution from his Roth IRA, tax- and penalty-free, to purchase it. Now he has saved years of rent payments in comparison to his peers. Tommie is way ahead of them, all because Mom and Dad hired him at the age of fourteen and gave him life skills that allowed him to gain a professional and financial advantage.

Now, MBE, you are building generational wealth. You are building this wealth all because of smart, Profit First tax strategy!

THE WORK OPPORTUNITY TAX CREDIT

As of this writing, the Work Opportunity Tax Credit (WOTC) has expired and been renewed again, as it has year after year. The WOTC is a federal tax credit created to give employers an incentive to hire individuals from targeted groups, particularly targeted groups who have historically faced difficulties gaining employment. Personally, I love the Work Opportunity Tax Credit. It generates opportunities for so many people who would not normally have access to employment. If used correctly, this credit not only changes lives; it also translates to significant tax savings for employers. The WOTC can change so many people's generational legacies.

This tax credit can be substantial. For example, at the time of this writing, if you are an entrepreneur who hires a disabled veteran with a service-connected disability who has been unemployed for a period of at least six months, you can get a tax credit of up to $9,600. Nice, right? This credit amount will vary depending on the target group that has been identified for the tax credit.

Target groups include:

- Veterans
- Long-term family assistance recipients who are members of a family that has received Temporary Assistance for Needy Families (TANF) benefits for at least eighteen consecutive months
- TANF recipients themselves
- Ex-felons
- Designated community residents
- Vocational rehabilitation referrals
- Supplemental Nutrition Assistance Program (SNAP) recipients
- Supplemental Security Income recipients
- Long-term unemployment recipients
- Summer Youth Employment Program recipients

The credit requires a certification from the applicable state workforce agency. This approval is granted by your state when you complete the IRS Form 8850 Pre-screening Notice and Certification Request for the Work Opportunity Tax Credit. To screen for this credit, our clients normally include the Form 8850 as part of their employment application. Check with your attorney to determine if there are any state laws that preclude you from doing this prior to establishing screening as a part of your procedures.

In addition to the Form 8850, you will also be required to submit one of the following forms to your state workforce agency:

a. ETA Form 9062, Conditional Certification, which the applicant would have received from a participating agency such as a Job Corps; or

b. ETA Form 9061, Individual Characteristics Form (ICF), if no conditional certification (self-certification) was received from a participating agency; or

c. ETA Form 9175, Long Term Unemployment Recipient Self-Attestation Form, if the job applicant is a qualified long-term unemployment recipient.

You may find the form 8850 on the IRS website. You may locate your state workforce agency at the Department of Labor's website.

As an employer, you must obtain certification that the candidate is a member of the targeted group before you may claim the credit. In addition, you must obtain certification that the individual is an eligible worker within twenty-eight days of the eligible worker's start date. You must also retain the certified individual as an employee for at least 120 hours.

The Work Opportunity Tax Credit has some limitations. For example, it is limited to the amount of business income tax liability or Social Security tax owed. If you are not able to utilize the full credit in the current year, you may carry it back for a refund or carry it forward to future years. If yours is a qualified tax-exempt organization, you are also eligible for the credit. However, the credit is limited to the amount of employer Social Security tax owed on wages paid to all employees for the period during which the credit is claimed.

MBE, THERE ARE SO MANY more tax strategies that you can employ. These are just some of my favorites. Of course, your personal situation will dictate which tax strategies are most pertinent to you. I highly recommend that you work with a tax accountant who specializes in high net worth taxation. I host *The Profit Talk* podcast. In this podcast, I regularly discuss tax strategies with our audiences. Join me sometime and listen in.

CHAPTER THIRTEEN

Embrace an Environment
of Continuous Improvement

KYM YANCEY, WHOM YOU MET in Chapter 11, had put a lot of work into creating his advertising proposal. Pfizer was launching a new product, and Kym was excited about the opportunity to be of service to them. When his proposal met his own highest standards, he submitted it. Pfizer, in turn, declined the proposal. Most people would have walked away in disappointment; however, Kym decided to do the opposite. He decided to call Kelly, his contact at Pfizer, to determine how they could have made this work. The phone rang and went to voicemail.

Kym left the following voicemail: "Hey Kelly, this is Kym. I'm giving you a buzz, calling to ask you for just a little help. You've already told me that you are passing on the proposal. So I'm not calling about that. What I am calling about, if you would be so gracious as to assist, is to ask if you would tell me what I did wrong. I just want to know going into this what I could, what I should have done. What I should have considered when putting together this proposal, you know, to make this work. So I'm just asking you to give me some feedback. It would help me in my personal development and my personal growth. I'd be deeply appreciative."

To Kym's surprise, Kelly returned his phone call. She explained that he didn't get the contract because his proposal was over budget by $15,000. Kelly said, "If it was $15,000 less, if you could trim some things off, we will go with that."

Kym made a few adjustments, redrafted Pfizer a package for $15,000 less, and got the deal.

Kym told me, "The key is that I was very authentic when I was saying this to her. I just really wanted to know where I had gone wrong."

Kym shared another story about submitting a proposal to a credit union to take care of their advertising. There were several other agencies bidding for the job. Kym's firm put a lot of time into the plan before submitting the documents. The woman in charge came back and informed Kym that they had decided not to go with his firm. The woman explained, "They loved your plan, Kym, but they decided not to go with you."

Again, Kym asked why. The woman said, "Your plan was inside of a little three-ring Office Depot binder with a little sticker on the outside. And that was your plan. Your competitor had a suede binder, beautiful. Their logo was embossed on the binder. They put it in a box with tissue paper and closed it and gave it to us. I mean, they beat you before we even read your proposal. Your proposal was better, but they killed you in the presentation, in what they presented to the market."

Kym then said to me, "That was the last time that happened."

The point of the matter, Kym explained, is to expect a rejection at some point. It's also so important to understand why, what you are up against, and why someone was chosen over you, as opposed to making assumptions.

I asked Kym what he thought about statistics that allude to the fact that sometimes, a rejection is a result of discrimination.

Kym said, "You don't want to spend any time in the things you're passed over for. You want to spend time in your positivity and in your uniqueness. Bring your enthusiasm to the opportunity. I want you to know there's a lot of positive opportunity out here, too. I mean, a ton of it. It's so easy to get caught up in that negative energy, that negative vibe. And I'm not talking about putting on rose-colored glasses. I'm not saying that at all. I'm saying that it's 'showtime' for you, and it's your moment. You get to decide what comes across in that moment. You get to make it what you want it to be and step into you—your uniqueness and who you are and what you are about. Those times when you're feeling like, *They might think my hair's too wild*—you might be thinking that, and they're thinking, *What a unique hairstyle she's got.*"

MBE, discrimination does happen, as you well know. However, don't dwell on the things you cannot change. Create your own possibility. Unearth the gold hidden in the "no." Always look for the learning opportunity. This is what will move you toward your goal.

NEVER STOP LEARNING

THE FUN PART OF LIVING is that, hopefully, you will never stop learning until the moment you die. This means that you will always have the opportunity to continue to learn something new, bring something new to market, and reinvent yourself.

MBE, always continue to learn; always continue to make yourself better; always continue to make your company better. Never be the same person you were a year ago. Go further; become a better version of you. Challenge your team to do the same. Continue to grow. Continue to become *better*.

Over the years, I have continually invested in my education. I've attended the American Institute of Certified Public Accountants tax school; invested in becoming an American Institute of Certified Tax Planners, Inc. Certified Tax Coach; and invested in becoming a Certified Profit First Professional. I always invested to become *more*. I want to be the best that I can be so that I can help my clients continue to grow. I want to guide others toward becoming better versions of themselves.

MBE, attend your trade conferences. Heck, attend conferences outside your trade. Allocate money to a reserve account each month so that you can make your annual trips. Read more books. Read books on different topics so that you are always expanding your mind and satisfying your curiosity. Never stop investing in your mind. Your mind is your biggest asset. I wish the kids I grew up with in my old neighborhood realized this. We should all be investing in our minds. This will move us much farther along the road, giving our children opportunities that we never had.

The great thing about problem-solving is, the more you do it, the better you get. Don't shy away from challenges; step up and solve them. See if you can figure them out before you hire a consultant. Always work on sharpening your mind. Take classes outside of your expertise. Take marketing classes, advertising classes, and sales classes that reach beyond your zone of genius. Learn how to mentor and develop others. If these skills are outside your area of expertise, learning them can only help you build a better version of yourself.

One of the best things I ever did for my business was learning every part of it. Don't get me wrong, I don't handle every part of my business; there just isn't time in the day for me to do that. If my company required me for every step of its operations, I would halt my company's growth and prevent it from meeting its commitments. However, in the event that any key person leaves my organization, I can simply step in and train another.

Knowing every part of my business means that I do not accept excuses. It also helps me recognize when things are broken and help my team brainstorm workable solutions. Knowing my business allows me to avoid being held hostage by anyone. MBE, know your business. Know every part of it. Document your processes. Sit with your team members and observe them doing their jobs. Create videos to use when you train new staff. These videos will allow new staff to learn more quickly so that they require less of your own or your managers' time. If they missed a step, they can simply watch the video again.

INVEST IN EFFICIENCY-BOOSTING TECHNOLOGIES

CONTINUALLY REVIEW YOUR BUSINESS'S PROCESSES. One thing that has always amazed me is the speed of development in technology. No business should be the same as it was the year before. Technological advancements are being brought to market so rapidly, we can all do our jobs more quickly and efficiently this year than we did last year.

I mentioned that we are in the midst of COVID-19 as I write this book. Without a moment's notice, many offices have been forced either to close up shop completely or go home and figure out how to operate remotely. To prevent the virus's spread, the Harris County judge (Harris County, representing Houston, is the largest county in Texas) mandated that everyone practice social distancing, and the government is only allowing essential businesses to stay open.

Luckily, at my company, Mariga CPA PLLC, we decided months ago to begin building our platform online. Although our company maintains a physical office space in Houston, many of our accountants are accustomed to working in the field, at client locations. I often work remotely just to make it easy to pick my children up from school.

In November, we hired our first remote employee from North Carolina and began communicating regularly as a team using an online meeting platform. And since we had already begun transitioning our operations in a way that allowed us to work anywhere, we were able to continue remotely and without difficulty when COVID-19 hit our nation.

Now that we have been social-distancing for a couple of months, I see no reason to invest in a larger office space. We can continue to operate remotely, and now that we can, we can also recruit the best talent from across the nation. Using technology, we are no longer limited by the square footage of our office space. MBE, constantly evaluate new technology. Constantly evaluate how you can make your operations more efficient. Do not allow your business to remain the same from year to year.

When things do not process well, or there is a slowdown in your operations, evaluate the operations. Take notes on your observations, figure out where there is a jam or what is deficient in quality, and tackle the issue head-on. I recommend observing your processes on at least an annual basis.

WE ARE ALL A WORK IN PROGRESS

FOSTER A CONTINUOUS IMPROVEMENT MENTALITY within your team. Reward your team for new ideas. I love the fifty-dollar gift certificates that you can award someone just for doing a great job. It's fifty dollars, but you would spend a whole lot more if you brought in a consultant to do the same work. Reward innovation, encourage innovation, and make a big deal out of it when new ideas are brought to the table in front of the entire team. A little praise can go far. Plus, it gets everyone motivated to participate.

One of the greatest joys I have experienced in creating my firm is getting to see the wonderful professionals my team members have become. My team has consistently given me the feedback that, though they work hard, they can now see themselves becoming so much more than they ever expected.

They are surprised at their well-honed problem-solving skills, and their greater ability to talk to entrepreneurs and CEOs with fancy titles. When they move on to the next point in their careers, which will happen, they will find their skill levels way above those of their peers. In fact, quite a few of my former employees go on to attain higher-level positions or are quickly promoted into management positions.

I teach my staff accounting and technical skills, but I also try to infuse the mix with some life skills. When they face stress or hard-to-deal-with clients, I walk them through the process of separating their emotions from the situation and thinking about the endgame. What, ultimately, is the best resolution? How can they kindly ask for the information they need and create a win-win environment in all of their interactions?

We do cross-reviews in my firm. A cross-review is when a peer-level staff member reviews another's work prior to it being brought to the manager for final review. This allows my team to cross-train in each other's jobs. It also allows them to gain a bit of managerial experience before they ever receive the official title. At our firm, we only promote those who act as managers to managerial positions.

Inspire your "A" players to be better and do more. Enroll them in classes that up-level their current job skills. When the "A" players return from training, have them teach the rest of the team. "A" players love to learn; they love to grow. I suspect that they enjoy growing more than they enjoy earning the extra money. Keep their minds sharp, keep them curious, and you will keep your company on the cutting edge.

Always take the time to get to know your team members. Take the opportunities to mentor them and give them feedback. Take the time to help develop them into better versions of themselves.

I love our team lunches. They are usually casual, on a Friday, and pretty laid-back. During these lunches, we discuss current events, client progress, and opportunities for improvement. My team loves it not only because they get lunch, but also because they get to know each other better. Informal relationships among staff help with staff retention. It is also much easier to give feedback for improvement when staff know that suggestions are coming from a place of kindness. We foster continuous improvement out of love for our craft.

CUSTOMER COMPLAINTS ARE OPPORTUNITIES FOR GROWTH

WATCH FOR CUSTOMER COMPLAINTS. SOMETIMES these complaints are not obvious. Sometimes a complaint is a sly request for you or your team to do an additional project. Sometimes it's a suggestion. Watch for these golden nuggets. They truly are gifts. Customer suggestions help you identify the *gap*. They tell you exactly what is broken in your current operation, what can be made better. Set up a customer recommendation box or send client experience surveys. Listening to your customers is a great way to get an advantage over your competitors.

Always look for the opportunities to make things better.

One thing I do to keep improving my business is define our main goals. After defining these goals, I ask myself: Are we are accomplishing our goals? If not, I ask: What must be in place for us to accomplish these goals? What is broken that must be fixed in order for us to accomplish our goals? The better the quality of the questions you ask yourself, the better the quality of your solutions will be. Ask yourself the hard questions. Dare to go deep to find the best answers.

Asking the hard questions about what is stopping you from meeting your end goals will help you generate the solutions that get where you want to go in the long-term. Embrace a mindset of curiosity and you will never stop reinventing yourself; you will never stop improving.

SEEK FIRST TO UNDERSTAND

When I asked Kym Yancey the question, "If you could offer one piece of advice to the next up-and-coming, rising MBE, what would it be?" his response focused on the importance of compassion and empathy.

"What I think is really powerful is this whole movement around mindfulness. You don't have to be in a rush to respond first. You'll never be accused of being too kind. It's so important. Stephen Covey's book, *The Seven Habits of Highly Effective People*, one that has been out for a while, is one of the best books of all time. The *seven* habits of highly effective people, but there's one that's most important: Seek first to understand before being understood.

"You don't have to be first, but make sure you understand the other person and where they're coming from. You know, everybody has beliefs, but back it down. If you feel yourself getting anxious, you feel yourself on the verge of snapping or you want to bark at somebody, your spouse or significant other, whatever the case may be, just take that breath, pull it back.

Bringing consciousness to your thoughts is so critical. It's so critical because people pick up on it.

"Be more compassionate—be more compassionate with yourself. Don't beat yourself up. Don't tear yourself down. There are enough forces out there that will do that for you for free. All you can do is do the best you can do with what you've got at the moment. Use the knowledge and insight that you have at that moment, in that time.

"Again, don't be so quick to respond. If you have a hot trigger, where all of a sudden you get upset or something, next thing you want is to back it down. There should be a sign to look for such as, *I got a hot trigger. I feel like saying something angry. I feel like snapping at somebody*; that's your sign to back it down, that's it, that's how you know. These things make a huge difference. They're going to make a huge difference in how you feel, how you approach your business, and your interactions with people."

NEXT STEPS

MBE, LET'S TAKE SOME TIME to brainstorm answers to a few questions. If you have a journal, it will be good to answer these questions in writing.

1. What changes do you see in your industry or the economy that may help you lead in your industry?

2. What skills are needed to lead this charge?

3. Is this an area in which you want to invest, in order to take your business to the next level?

4. What is the return on investment if you decide to invest in this area?

CHAPTER FOURTEEN

Create a Bold New Legacy

JERRY WON MADE IT CLEAR to his parents when he was a teenager that he would not study medicine, nor earn a living doing anything traditional. Although he flirted with the prospect of law school and eventually earned his MBA, Jerry was not going to allow the community to define his vision of success by a limited set of options. Unlike many of the traditional Asian families he grew up around, families who believed their choices were limited to a list of finite options, Jerry understood that the world was full of infinite possibilities and that he could create more. While systemic and cultural influences suggested that one should be a good employee, take a paycheck, and work toward a pension, Jerry understood that though this system might work for some, he was going down his own path.

Jerry had read a lot of business books and listened to a ton of business podcasts, but noticed that few people who looked like him sat in the guest chair *or* the host chair. He observed that the show hosts and their producers seemed to have no desire to ensure that their guest lists were diverse, much less any sense of urgency about changing their overwhelmingly white formats. Though there was nothing fundamentally wrong with the advice from a content perspective, these white hosts and their guests had no idea what it meant to grow up in an ethnic-minority family. Even if a white host was really smart, motivated, and famous, their way of handling a whole array of topics just did not work for someone like Jerry.

For Jerry, the only way to combat this was to provide his community with their own hope and inspiration through his own actions. He would give others hope so that they, too, could do the same.

That's the reason why Jerry started the *Dear Asian American* podcast, which showcases different avenues of Asian-American life, identity, and storytelling. The best episodes feature people who, despite being very talented and accomplished, are not being featured on mainstream podcasts. His guests are often overlooked because they don't look like the traditional American picture of success; mainstream media in the U.S. doesn't appear to believe that non-white, non-traditionally successful people have the authority to speak on any topic. The podcast features stories that Jerry always wished he had access to growing up, stories that provide inspiration, motivation, and role models.

Jerry understands that developing the right mindset is key. People need to believe that they are capable, that they have the right and ability to thrive in doing whatever they set their mind to. His guests and their stories provide the role models and narratives his audience needs to grow their own wings.

When I asked Jerry the same question I asked all the entrepreneurs I interviewed for this book, "If you could offer one piece of advice to the next up-and-coming, rising MBE, what would it be?" he replied: "Focus on the things that people will talk about at your funeral. Last time I checked, we don't put company logos, cars, and houses on tombstones or in coffins. People who show up to funerals show up because you made an impact in their lives. I know we're talking about business, but business at the end of the day is a bunch of transactions between human beings. If you focus on the impact that you want to have left on your customers, your members, your employees, and then on yourself, I think that will help you clarify what the next steps are.

"It's easier for you to attain financial goals and achievements when everything else aligns and everything else seems right. This goes back to your why. Why are you doing any of this? You buy the biggest house on the block. Somebody is going to build a bigger one. You buy the newest car. Next year it's old. We wanted $1,000,000 in sales this year, great. Somebody is doing $5,000,000. Are you going to let those metrics determine your value and worth as an entrepreneur and as a human being?

"My advice is, focus on what you want to accomplish. Give yourself the grace to change your mission. If you're going through different life stages—marriage, children, divorce, education, health—let it change. That's the beauty of life, that you're doing it for yourself. We're on a podcast talking about a book.

"So, I'll leave it with the book metaphor. If your life is a book, there are many, many, many blank pages. Who's going to write it? How do you want that book to end? 'Cause that's on you. You can change how it is told, and what that story is. If you've had ugly experiences in your life, as we all have, do you dedicate chapters upon chapters to that, focusing on it, or do you just write a blurb? Make it a mention and focus on how you recovered from it. It is really important to figure out and train yourself on how you're going to tell the stories of things that have happened. Also, figure out a strategy for how you're going to write the rest of your book because if you don't, somebody's going to write that story for you, and you're probably not going to be very happy with that ending."

The primary mission of Jerry's podcast is to tackle the dismantling of systemic racism by providing a platform for Asian Americans. Instead of eliminating their voices, he strove to amplify them.

Jerry Won's company, Just Like Media, is now home to multiple entries on Apple's list of Top 100 U.S. Podcasts. *Dear Asian American* has helped form coalitions and build movements. For Jerry, its greatest gift is that he will never know the true impact he will make on the world, in perpetuity, by having decided to create something.

What legacy will you leave, MBE? What impact will you have on the community and the world around you?

You have been given all the tools you need to now run a wildly profitable business. You are entering new rooms, creating new opportunities. You have set up your bank accounts; you are making bimonthly transfers. Your profits are growing, your lifestyle is improving, and you will one day be able to drop cash for that new car and drive away debt-free.

How will you give back to your community? What impact will you make? How will the world remember you when you are gone?

You don't have to wait to have an impact. You can start *today*. Each one, teach one. Start by giving a copy of this book to a fellow MBE. I am sure you know of someone who might need it. Let's start with elevating our people to a greater level.

Start eradicating entrepreneurial poverty in your own backyard. Start with someone who looks like you, someone in your neighborhood, town, or city.

When you help someone else to best their best, we all win as a society.

I am so proud of where my Profit First clients have gone and what they have become. My initial meeting with a client is often with a business owner who is barely scraping by, much less earning any profit. After implementing Profit First for a year or so, such a client might bring home $500,000 a year in combined profit, tax, and owner's compensation, not only elevating their own personal lifestyle, but changing the legacy of their children and grandchildren. It is so fulfilling for me to know that, together, we have changed a family for generations to come.

Harriet Tubman escaped slavery. Between 1850 and 1860, she returned to the South time and time again, carrying a torch that lit our way to freedom.

This torch is now yours to carry. You call the shots. You determine our future. Create a legacy that makes us proud. Take your profit first. Our future depends on it.

MBE, now that you know how to run a wildly profitable, cash flow-positive minority business enterprise, what will your impact be? How will the world remember you? I'd love to hear about the legacy that you are leaving. Email me today: smariga@ SusanneMariga.com.

APPENDIX 1

Glossary of Key Terms

CAPs (current allocation percentages): CAPs are the current percentages you use to allocate money to your various accounts. A profit CAP of 5% means that you will transfer 5% of the balance in your Income Account to your Profit Account twice a month.

Debt snowball: Coined by Dave Ramsey, the "debt snowball" is an approach to tackling debt that pays off your smallest debts first. This helps you build momentum toward tackling your larger debts and achieving financial freedom.

Endowment effect: Studies in behavioral economics have shown that we tend to value what we own more highly than what we don't. This is called the "endowment effect."

GAAP (Generally Accepted Accounting Principles): Generally Accepted Accounting Principles are a set of accounting standards and procedures used by most businesses. GAAP assumes that Sales - Expenses = Profit, thereby treating profit as an afterthought.

Loss aversion: Related to the endowment effect, loss aversion is the psychological phenomenon that makes us resistant to giving up what we already have, even if it is for an equal or greater gain.

Minority business enterprise (MBE): A for-profit business located in the United States whose ownership and control is 51% or greater by member(s) who are considered of a minority group. This racial demographic includes Asian Indian, Asian-Pacific, Black, Hispanic, and Native American. Certification by the National Minority Supplier Development Council (NMSDC) or by a local MBE program administered by a city, county, or state may require legal residency or U.S. citizenship.

National Minority Supplier Development Council (NMSDC): NMSDC is one of country's leading corporate membership organizations that is dedicated to advancing the opportunities for certified minority business enterprises and connects them to corporate members Its corporate membership includes many of the largest public and privately-owned companies, as well as healthcare companies, colleges, and universities. You may contact NMSDC at https://nmsdc.org.

8(a) Business Development Program: A program administered by the U.S. Small Business Administration (SBA), whose goal is to provide a level playing field for small businesses owned by socially and economically disadvantaged peoples or entities. The benefits of the program are that it allows certified entities to complete for set-aside and sole-sourced contracts;

form joint ventures with established businesses through the SBA's Mentor-Protege Program; and receive management and technical assistance including business training, counseling, marketing assistance, and high-level executive development.

OPEX: Short for Operating Expenses. In the Profit First system, you should be paying all your bills out of your OPEX account.

Pareto Principle: Otherwise known as the 80/20 rule, the Pareto Principle states that 80% of effects come from 20% of causes. In other words, 80% of your revenue tends to come from 20% of your clients. To further boost your revenue, try to replicate and do more business with this top 20%.

Parkinson's Law: C. Northcote Parkinson's adage that work expands to fill the available time is the same tendency your business has to use up all available resources. This is also known as induced demand, and is the main reason why you need to stow away your profit before you find ways to spend it.

Profit assessment: Income statements and balance sheets can be tedious and confusing. The instant assessment is a tool that gives you a quick, clear view of the current financial health of your business.

Profit First Professional (PFP): PFPs are certified accounting professionals who are well-versed in the Profit First system. To find one, go to https://www.ProfitFirstProfessionals.com.

Real Revenue: When performing the Profit Assessment, we use Real Revenue as an alternative to gross profit. In the cases where there is a significant use of subcontractors and/or materials, those costs are subtracted from income to drive the "true revenue" (i.e., Real Revenue) that the company generates. Calculations to gross profits in traditional accounting can vary based on different interpretations. The objective of Real Revenue is to simplify the calculations variable.

Sales – Expenses = Profit: The traditional accounting formula that we are going to flip to achieve profitability: Sales – Profit = Expenses.

Survival trap: When you operate your business check to check, you'll find yourself in the survival trap, doing anything to generate revenue—even when it goes against your company's vision and is outside the bounds of your top clients' needs.

TAPs (target allocation percentages): The ideal percentage of revenue you should eventually aim to allocate to Profit, Tax, Owner's Compensation, and Operating Expenses. You will gradually increase your CAPs toward your TAPs for Profit, Tax, and Owner's Compensation. You will gradually decrease your CAPs for OPEX.

Wedge: A system to gradually upgrade your lifestyle as your income grows.

Woman-owned business enterprises (WBEs): Businesses that are at least 51% owned by a woman or women. You may receive this certification from the Women's Business Enterprise National Council (WBENC) or through a program administered by a city, county, or state. These certifying agencies may require legal residency or U.S. citizenship. If you are an MBE and your business has female ownership of 51% or more, you may also qualify as a WBE.

Women's Business Enterprise National Council (WBENC): A 501(c)(3) non-profit that provides certification to women-owned businesses throughout the United States and offers programs and resources to help women-owned businesses thrive. This organization is supported by corporate and government members who are dedicated to supplier diversity and investing in the development of women-owned businesses and suppliers.

ACKNOWLEDGMENTS

I AM GRATEFUL FOR THE thought leadership of so many who contributed to the creation of this book. I want to thank Mike Michalowicz for this opportunity, and for the creation of the brilliant Profit First concept. This cash management methodology has changed so many family legacies, and I am so proud to be a part of the mission to eradicate entrepreneurial poverty.

I want to thank my developmental editor, Anjanette Harper, who helped me cut and rephrase countless sentences to create the book I am proud of today. Thanks to Zoë Bird for copy editing and Choi Messer for typesetting. I also want to thank our intern, Katherine Huggins, for her tireless research of statistics; Rachel Fragd, my brilliant assistant, who schedules interviews and manages to keep everything together; and Angi Lewis, for the beautiful cover photo.

I'd like to thank my wonderful parents, Connie Jenkins and Roy Chan, without whose wisdom and sacrifice this book would not be possible. The gift of their wisdom is invaluable.

Finally, I'd like to thank, my husband, Jeffrey Mariga, for his patience in allowing me to live out my dream; and my loyal sidekicks, Florence and Emmanuel Mariga, for their eager participation in life's adventures (which become the basis of the stories I tell).

CONTACT US!

Visit our resources page at https://www.SusanneMariga.com.

If you need additional assistance with implementing Profit First, or would like to connect with Susanne for speaking engagements, contact SMariga@SusanneMariga.com.

To learn more about Profit First accounting and tax services, go to https://www.MarigaCPA.com.

FOLLOW US!

https://Facebook.com/marigacpa/
https://Linkedin.com/company/mariga-cpa-pllc

CPSIA information can be obtained
at www.ICGtesting.com
Printed in the USA
BVHW052152141022
649471BV00008B/579